GOD'S NOT DEAD 2

STAND WITH GOD

A 40-DAY Devotional

ROBERT NOLAND

BroadStreet
P U B L I S H I N G

BroadStreet Publishing Group, LLC
Racine, Wisconsin, USA
BroadStreetPublishing.com

GOD'S NOT DEAD 2

Based on the motion picture *God Is Not Dead 2* by Pure Flix Entertainment. All content from the movie used by permission.

Published in association with the literary agency WTA Services LLC, Franklin, TN

ISBN-13: 978-1-4245-5198-9 (softcover)
ISBN-13: 978-1-4245-5199-6 (e-book)

Cover design by Chris Garborg at www.garborgdesign.com
Typesetting by Katherine Lloyd at www.theDESKonline.com

Stock or custom editions of BroadStreet Publishing titles may be purchased in bulk for educational, business, ministry, fundraising, or sales promotional use. For information, please e-mail info@broadstreetpublishing.com.

Printed in the United States of America

16 17 18 19 20 5 4 3 2

Contents

Introduction

Mark 1:35 tells us Jesus got up early in the morning and went away alone to pray. One of the most life-changing spiritual disciplines you can invest in is a daily and dedicated time alone with God. No distractions, no devices or noise, and no one else around. Here are a few steps for success in utilizing this book:

1. Decide to commit.
Purpose to use this book for the next forty days, setting aside the time to make a habit of engaging with the words contained here. If you miss a day, just pick back up. Don't quit—commit.

2. Pick a time.
While spending a few moments alone with God first thing in the morning is best to set the pace for your day, choose when will be optimum for your schedule. You may need to experiment a bit, but pick a time and stick with it.

3. Choose a place.
You need a quiet and peaceful setting. Get away from distractions. Turn off the phone. The place is crucial for you to be focused and comfortable as you engage with God.

4. Read.
Take in the content—every word. Carefully read the Bible verses. If you prefer to use your own version of Scripture each day, feel free to do so.

5. Journal.

Journaling space is included with each daily reading. Answer any closing questions, then write out anything you hear from God or feel you need to express. Journaling is a powerful tool He can use to help you process your spiritual walk.

6. Pray.

Allow time to speak with God and tell Him everything as you would a best friend. If you have never invested in personal prayer, the next forty days could revolutionize your spiritual growth.

7. Listen and obey.

Close your time with a quiet moment to hear God speak. Then obey what you hear and "walk out" what He tells you each day. The goal is to complete these forty days and allow Jesus to change your life!

> "Here's what I want you to do: Find a quiet, secluded place so you won't be tempted to role-play before God. Just be there as simply and honestly as you can manage. The focus will shift from you to God, and you will begin to sense his grace." (Matthew 6:6 MSG)

HOPE AND GRACE

A new day dawns over Hope Springs. A young woman wearing a Hadleigh University sweatshirt slips out her front door with a steaming mug of coffee cupped in her hands. She sits down on the top step of the porch. Meet Grace Wesley, voted Teacher of the Year by the students at the high school where she teaches history. She reflects her namesake well— gracious, humble, and quite wise for her young age. She also loves Jesus … and her grandpa.

As the sun peeks over the world, Grace takes in the beauty of creation from the heart of one who knows her Creator well. She soaks in the quiet moment like a cleansing breath, takes another sip of coffee, and then heads back inside to start her day.

Grace finishes making some hot tea to place on a tray with toast, oatmeal, and blueberries, all in carefully measured portions. She picks up the picture-perfect breakfast and heads toward a bedroom.

Meet Gramps: Walter Wesley. While his body is failing, his mind and spirit are strong and quick. "Morning, Grace. I told you … you don't have to keep doing this," he says lovingly, referring to yet another meal delivered to his bedside.

Grace sets the tray down and smiles. "Gramps, *this is* the best part of my day."

Walter grins. "Yeah, well, I'm not going to be around here forever, you know. You might want to think about finding another guy to have breakfast with."

Grace lets the remark about his declining health slide, but not the humor. "Okay Gramps, I'll work on it."

As Walter contemplates his oatmeal, he decides to attempt a ploy he's not at all sure will work, but he certainly wants to try. "Grace, I love your cooking, honey, but how about I take you out for some bacon and eggs this morning? My treat."

She smiles. "Not after your last cholesterol test. Besides, I have a few papers to grade before my staff meeting."

Walter refuses to concede. "I'm eighty-one years old. Bacon isn't going to be what kills me!"

Grace leans over and kisses him on his forehead. "You're eighty-two … and nice try. See you when I get home, Gramps."

———·———

There is a simple, yet honest beauty alive in Grace's life.

> The Mighty One, God, the Lord, speaks and summons the earth from the rising of the sun to where it sets. From Zion, perfect in beauty, God shines forth. Our God comes and will not be silent…. (Psalm 50:1–3 NIV)

In God's creation, He does shine in beauty through the majesty painted before our eyes, and His presence is felt through the rays of sunshine on our faces. In those moments, we can hear Him whisper to our souls. Even in the silence, God is not silent!

No matter how busy life may get or how chaotic circumstances may become, there is a childlike simplicity to be found in every sunrise and sunset. There in the luminescent glow of the dawn or the subdued blues of dusk lies a deep knowing that God is indeed in control. His presence is emblazoned across the sky for any and all to see His handiwork.

For Grace, a high school teacher and caretaker of her elderly grandfather, no matter what challenges life brings her way, the certainty of her heavenly Father being beside her in each new day gives her comfort and security.

Little does she know, however, that a storm is coming and she will need all the peace she has stored up during her morning meetings with God. Life is about to throw her into a battle like none she has ever faced before.

When was the last time you sat quietly and watched the sunrise, expressing appreciation for God?

When was the last time you stopped to soak up some moments of solitude, to watch the sunset, thanking God for another day of life?

If your answer is that life is just too busy, this may be the perfect reminder to unplug for a few minutes and soak up some sun—and some Son.

In your journal, write down your most difficult challenges in life right now. Then write down a few of your greatest blessings. Ask God to show you how those blessings can give you the hope and grace to face the world by His side.

GRIEF INTO BELIEF

Sixteen-year-old Brooke Thawley trudges down the stairs into the kitchen. She's cute enough to be a cheerleader and smart enough to be captain of the debate team, but she belongs to neither. Her demeanor and countenance suggest she is carrying quite a heavy burden, especially for someone her age. She asks her dad, "Can you drive Marlene and me to school?"

Richard Thawley, a midforties businessman, is methodically packing his briefcase at the kitchen table. Staunch and all business, he answers, "No time today." Seeing the look on her face, he adds, "We're all upset, Brooke. But we need to move on. You especially need to."

She hears those words—again—and responds with a simple nod.

Dressed in yoga gear and holding on to every day of thirty-nine for all she's worth, Catherine Thawley rushes in and grabs a protein shake from the fridge. Tagging on to the conversation, she adds, "Honey, you're a junior now. It's your make-or-break year, so there's no room for self-pity."

As Brooke's frustration grows, she makes her way out the front door to find her BFF (best friend forever), Marlene, waiting there. She is all smiles until she sees Brooke's expression. "Hey, are you—? Whoa! Rough morning?"

"You know my parents," Brooke says as the two start down the sidewalk.

"Did you try to talk with them? Or are they just not going to deal with it?"

Brooke shrugs. "They're over it and think I should just get over it too."

Marlene tries to reassure her friend. "Maybe they just need a little more time."

Just then, Brooke's mom pulls up and through the car window says, "I'm serious, honey. You need to get focused, or you can say good-bye, Stanford, hello, Somewhere State. What would your brother want you to do?"

Brooke just keeps walking, "Got it, Mom."

———·———

Carter was Brooke's brother. He left her all too soon. His death created a void in their family that no one knew how to deal with … so they just didn't.

A devastating loss needs to be both felt and dealt with properly to bring healing. Our Western culture often doesn't allow people an opportunity to grieve. This causes many, even inside a close family, to take an every-man-for-himself approach.

Grief is an inevitable fact of life. The loss of loved ones will impact us in serious ways. But there are two kinds of grief—*without* hope and *with* hope.

And now, dear brothers and sisters, we want you to know what will happen to the believers who have died so you will not grieve like people who have no hope. For since we believe that Jesus died and was raised to life again, we also believe that when Jesus returns, God will bring back with him the believers who have died. (1 Thessalonians 4:13–14 NLT)

The apostle Paul clearly addressed the difference in grief with hope in his letter to the Thessalonian Christians. Notice he didn't say to *not* grieve at all.

While most mental health professionals agree that denial, anger, bargaining, depression, and acceptance are stages of grief most people go through, there is no timetable for how long each of these last. People struggling with grief can get "stuck" in any one of these emotional spots for quite a long time. But most eventually arrive at acceptance and healing in due time.

For the Christian who dies, heaven is a sudden reality. For the Christian who suffers the loss of a loved one who knows Christ, certainly the pain is very real, but as the apostle Paul stated in today's verse, we can know the person is safe in the arms of God. Our grief can lead to hope and even greater belief. How much more real is heaven when someone you know has gone there!

If you have dealt with the loss of a loved one, write down in your journal the emotions you felt (or are still feeling now), evaluating where you are. Have you moved forward in hope, or are you stuck? Help is always available. Secondly, whether you have lost a loved one or not, write down why you know you can have hope for yourself. Then thank God for His promises and your place in heaven.

THE PRESENT
OF PRESENCE

Grace sits alone in the coffee shop after school, sipping a latte and grading papers. She looks up as Brooke approaches her table. Grace, being an observant and concerned teacher, noticed something was not quite right with Brooke at school. When she asked, the teenager just gave the predictable, nonchalant answer: "I'm fine."

Brooke sits down and jumps right in. "I lied. I'm not fine." A deep discussion ensues and we pick it up in the middle …

"Are you sure you're being fair to your parents?" Grace asks.

"Trust me. They're over it. And they expect me to be over it too. As far as they're concerned, Carter's gone forever. And now, I'm just trying to make sense of all this … And life? I don't even know what it means anymore. My parents are totally materialistic. Marlene's the only friend I have that isn't completely self-absorbed, and I'm just, well … lost."

Brooke continues, "The only thing I know for sure is that I'm never going to see my brother again. Everybody's asked me if there is anything they can do. But the truth is, no one can do anything because the only thing I really want is just five more minutes to tell my brother how I felt about him."

Grace, knowing where the conversation needs to go for Brooke's sake, asks, "Did your brother believe there was something more?"

"I don't know."

"Do you believe there's something more?" Grace inquires, a little bolder.

Brooke pauses, thinking, not knowing how to answer.

Grace assures her, "Every person reaches a point in their life when they ask themselves this question. There's nothing wrong with you asking it now too."

"So I'm not weird?" Brooke asks, trying to risk a smile.

"Weird? No. Unique? Yes," Grace counters.

Brooke is deep in thought now. "Nothing ever gets to you." She pauses. "How do you do that?"

Grace answers humbly but confidently, "Jesus."

———

As He was teaching His disciples about the coming Holy Spirit, Christ made an amazing statement and encouraging promise for His followers.

> "I am leaving you with a gift—peace of mind and heart. And the peace I give is a gift the world cannot give. So don't be troubled or afraid." (John 14:27 NLT)

Jesus defines and distinguishes His brand of peace as being different from the circumstantial counterfeit available from the world. God's peace isn't dependent on life going right or wrong, the ups and downs, but rather solely on Him. His peace remains steady, strong, and supportive regardless of any situation.

The daily news feed brings us the details of battles all over the world—personal to political. Meanwhile, our minds and hearts send us constant signals of our own turmoil going on within. This can make the concept of true peace start to feel like just a pipe dream. The chaos we experience in so many areas of life can make this deep need seem like a distant mirage. There is even a chance that, for so many today, something or someone may be holding their peace hostage, demanding that it be handed over in trade for fear, fret, or futility.

Likely, if you were to ask the man on the street to define peace, you would hear an answer that describes the absence of something—no war, violence, or strife.

Jesus—the Prince of Peace—is never about the *absence* of anything, but about the powerful *presence* of Him!

When life seems to be pushing and pulling you, robbing you of your peace, don't hope for the circumstances to change or leave. Rather, pray for the presence of God to *overpower*, *overwhelm*, and *overcome* you in your circumstances.

God's peace is *unexplainable*, *unavoidable*, and *unquestionable*. It just *is*—and when it is, you know it, you feel it, and you sense Him right there with you.

In your journal, write down your top five burdens, challenges, or struggles right now. Next, in the quiet stillness, ask God to bring His peace over you, your heart, and to come right into the middle of those situations. Invite Him in so you won't be troubled or afraid.

FINDING FOREVER

M rs. Thawley is on her way out the door for another busy day—designer purse and all. She sees a large truck pull up in front of the house and calls out, "Brooke, the people from that charity place are here to pick up your brother's things. Can you make sure they get everything?"

Her mother's calloused words feel like a slap in the face. Brooke quietly heads up the stairs toward her brother's room. She looks around at the many stacks of boxes that to her are all that is left of him, realizing every trace of Carter is about to be gone.

The Salvation Army workers begin to come in and out of the room, removing memory after memory, each one taking another piece of her heart. Brooke just sits, feeling very alone, staring far away, as Carter's things disappear forever.

One of the workers walks back in and politely says, "Well, that's the last of it." Brooke just looks down and nods. Then the lady adds, "As I was loading one of the boxes onto the truck, I noticed this. I thought you might want to keep it."

Brooke looks up to see a Bible. As Brooke takes it from her, the lady offers, "I'm sorry for your loss."

Brooke is mildly shocked as she slowly opens the front cover and reads Carter's words written there …

MY COMMITMENT TO CHRIST:

But as many as received Him, to them He gave the right to become children of God, *even* to those who believe in His name. (John 1:12 NASB)

CARTER THAWLEY – May 15

Brooke just keeps staring at her brother's name under the strange, cryptic language about Jesus, running her fingers over the page. *What does this mean?* she thinks, feeling like she has discovered not only a confidential message about her brother but a new connection to him she can now hold on to.

Brooke begins to read, engrossed in the pages that her brother read, even in his last days. Deep in her soul, she senses something odd, but awesome … *hope.*

———·———

For everyone has sinned; we all fall short of God's glorious standard. Yet God freely and graciously declares that we are righteous. He did this through Christ Jesus when he freed us from the penalty for our sins. For God presented Jesus as the sacrifice for sin. People are made right with God when they believe that Jesus sacrificed his life, shedding his blood. … God did this to demonstrate his righteousness, for he himself is fair and just, and he declares sinners to be right in his sight when they believe in Jesus. (Romans 3:23–26 NLT)

The gospel really is quite simple, even though we often try to make God's message complex. Because of our built-in disobedience to Him, we were all born knowing how to be disrespectful, selfish, and all about "me."

God, in His mercy, sent Jesus, His only Son, to die once and for all as a sacrifice for our sin. He died so we would not have to. But God's love gives us the free choice to accept this truth—or not. He does not force His way on anyone.

How about you? Is God alive in *your* life? Are you ready to be "freed from the penalty for sin"? The prayer Carter prayed when he wrote that note in his Bible is for everyone. The gospel is available to you today—right now. You can pray this for yourself:

Dear God, I know I have disobeyed you and need your forgiveness. I choose to turn from my sin and receive the gift of salvation and eternal life you are offering me. Thank you for dying for me, saving me, and changing my life. In Jesus' name. Amen.

If you prayed that prayer, tell a pastor/priest, Christian friend, or family member. Let someone know. Salvation isn't a secret!

If you are confident you are a Christ follower, share the gospel with a "Brooke" in your life—someone who is hurting and needs to hear about the love of God.

In your journal, just like Carter, write down the date of your salvation as best you can recall. If that is today—congratulations! Then thank God for His forgiveness and faithfulness.

THE PRICE OF PEACE

Grace has written several quotes on the board in her classroom:

"There are many causes I would die for. There is not one I would kill for." —Mahatma Gandhi

"Do to us what you will. And we shall continue to love you." —Dr. Martin Luther King Jr.

She continues her lecture. "So peaceful nonviolence comes first in India, under Gandhi and, later, here in the United States under Dr. King and others as a means of achieving civil rights. But what makes nonviolence so radical is its unwavering commitment to a nonthreatening approach—not just initially, but in the face of escalating persecution by the opposing force."

Brooke, highly tuned in from the time she spent reading Carter's Bible, raises her hand. Grace nods for her to speak. "Isn't that sort of like what Jesus meant when He said that we should love our enemies?"

The question catches Grace completely off-guard. She's surprised to hear a quote from Jesus in her classroom, but especially from Brooke.

Carefully gathering her thoughts, Grace answers, "Well ... yes. The writer of the gospel of Matthew recorded Jesus as saying: 'You have heard it said, "Love your neighbor and hate your enemy," but I tell you, love your enemies and pray for those who persecute you, that you may be children of your father in heaven.' This does indicate a commitment to nonviolence. Dr. King confirmed the link, describing his inspiration from Scripture by saying, 'Christ furnished the spirit and motivation, while Gandhi furnished the method.'"

A young man everyone knows to be sarcastic *and* apathetic calls out, "Except it didn't work. Jesus got himself killed. Everybody knows that."

A few students laugh, while one slips his cell phone from his pocket and begins to quietly text a message.

Grace, respectful as always, offers a response. "So did Dr. King. I guess it depends on how you measure success. Both started movements that survive to this day, even though both paid the ultimate price for commitment to their ideals."

The same kid fires back, "I still wouldn't do it."

Grace continues, "Not very many people have that kind of courage. But I'm grateful for those that do—for those who are willing to stand for what they believe."

Grace has no way of knowing that—all too soon—those very words will test her own faith. Meanwhile, Brooke is deep in thought, her soul stirring with this new paradigm she is discovering.

———·———

When we read the Gospels, an important factor to keep in mind is the Jews were looking for the Messiah to come as a military leader to administer justice and free them from oppression. They were thinking a sword-brandishing warrior on a white horse, not a simple carpenter who taught of peace. These were not the words they were looking to hear.

> "But to you who are listening I say: Love your enemies, do good to those who hate you, bless those who curse you, pray for those who mistreat you. If someone slaps you on one cheek, turn to them the other also. If someone takes your coat, do not withhold your shirt from them. Give to everyone who asks you, and if anyone takes what belongs to you, do not demand it back. Do to others as you would have them do to you." (Luke 6:27–31 NIV)

The kingdom of God has always run in full opposition to the world's ways. Man says to hate the haters; God says to love the haters. Man says to get revenge; God says to repent. Man says to take; God says to give. Man says you only give to get; God says you get so you can give.

Like the young man in Grace's classroom, many people are always going to think the ways of God are weak and pointless, much like Professor Radisson did—at least up until his final moments of life. But those such as Josh, Martin, Amy, and, even now, Brooke, will seek the truth.

Are you willing to stand up for what you believe? Do you, as Grace said, have that kind of courage?

In your journal, write out a personal prayer, asking God to give you the boldness to bless, give, serve, and love as He loves. Use today's Scripture passage as your guide.

THE ULTIMATE QUESTION

Martin Yip, the university student from China whom we first met in Professor Radisson's classroom, is walking quickly up to the parking lot at St. James Church. As Reverend Dave is walking out of the building, he sees Martin coming toward him.

"Are you Pastor Dave?" the young man asks.

"That's me," the reverend answers.

"I am Martin Yip. My friend Josh Wheaton said you might be able to answer my questions … about God."

Reverend Dave displays his classic, playful smirk and responds, "Well, that most definitely falls within my job description." Martin pulls a handful of handwritten pages from his messenger bag, prompting a slightly confused look from Dave. "How many questions have you got?"

"So far? One hundred and forty-seven," Martin answers. Dave chuckles, causing Martin to ask, "Is something wrong? Josh encouraged me to write my questions down and to make them as comprehensive as possible."

Reverend Dave smiles knowingly and quips, "Of course he

did. I'll have to thank Josh the next time I see him. Come on with me. So, what's your first question?"

Flashback to the classroom where Professor Radisson and Josh Wheaton are in the final moments of their heated exchange and the professor has just admitted he indeed hates God for what has happened in his life. Josh then calmly asked the question, "How can you hate someone if they don't exist?" That very moment sealed Martin's decision to confirm what he was feeling deep in his soul.

So when Josh turned to the rows of university students and said, "They get to choose. Is God dead?" it was like he drew a line in the sand. Martin swallowed hard, put away his notepad, stood up first, and declared, "God is *not* dead." His courage opened up the floodgate as student after student stood and declared the same: "God is *not* dead!"

After class, as Martin caught Josh on the stairwell, he said, "Your decision to prove God is not dead has affected me greatly. Yes, it has changed everything. I have decided to follow Jesus."

From that moment, Martin's life has been immersed in learning and experiencing all he can about his new life.

———·———

When Jesus came to the region of Caesarea Philippi, he asked his disciples, "Who do people say that the Son of Man is?" "Well," they replied, "some say John the Baptist, some say Elijah, and others say Jeremiah or one of the other prophets." Then he asked them, "But who do you say I am?" Simon Peter answered, "You are the

Messiah, the Son of the living God." Jesus replied, "You are blessed, Simon son of John, because my Father in heaven has revealed this to you. You did not learn this from any human being." (Matthew 16:13–17 NLT)

There was confusion amongst the people early on, even among His own disciples, about who Jesus truly was. Was He John the Baptist returned from the grave after his execution? Or was He one of the Old Testament prophets coming back for "round two"? Men were trying to identify Jesus as another man, when He was actually God Himself!

Jesus knew His disciples had to come to their own conclusion about Him. On this day, it was Peter's turn. He came to the same decision that Martin did in Radisson's classroom— God is alive, and Jesus is who He says He is.

Each person must make their own decision and "own" their own faith. No one should talk you into it, so no one can talk you out of it. As Jesus told Peter, "You didn't learn this truth from a human, but from God. He reveals the truth to hearts."

Is your faith your own? Do you feel you inherited it from someone or maybe felt pressure at some point in your life to believe? All that matters right now is who *you* say Jesus is— for you.

Like Martin, this is your call. No one will hitch a ride to heaven. When Jesus asks you, *Who do you say that I am?* what is your answer?

In your journal, write down your honest answer. Next, write down any and every reason why and how you know your faith is your own.

DIVERTING DOUBTS

When we first met frazzled and frustrated Amy, she had ambushed *Duck Dynasty*'s favorite couple, Willie and Korie Robertson, in front of a church. In classic Amy fashion, she asked them about killing ducks *and* praying to Jesus, while disgusted and mocking it all. As we might expect, Willie walked away completely unfazed by her attitude.

But her young world was soon rocked when, in the exam room, her doctor broke the news that she had cancer. Teetering between denial and devastation, she struggled with both life and death. Then, finally, when she went to a Christian concert for yet another impromptu interview, she found herself being prayed for. When we last saw our favorite blogger, she was sporting a fresh and quite peaceful smile.

Fast-forward to now—Amy receives the miraculous news that she can start a new chapter of life because her cancer is officially in remission. So, she's back at the keyboard and digging into controversy once again.

On this night, Amy is camped out alone in the back corner of the coffee shop. She holds her phone up and hits the record button on her voice memo app. "It amazes me how we, as human beings, think. When I was battling for my life, I was willing to hold on to anything … including God. Even though I didn't really believe in Him until that moment, I was convinced that I felt Him—but now that I'm officially in remission? I find myself questioning everything … including His existence. But how does God feel about all this? So effective immediately, this blog is the personal diary of one woman's exploration of faith on her own terms—cancer-free."

———·———

While we in the Christian community often attempt to shy away from expressing doubt and voicing faith struggles, here is the one problem with this mind-set: we all have them! Rather than hiding or ignoring our struggles and questions, what if we joined Amy and got brutally honest about how we feel and what we think? What if, rather than causing us to become disillusioned and walk away, this honest dialogue actually reinforced our faith? What if voicing doubt to one another created strength in our belief?

Doubt and struggle begin as thoughts. If entertained there and allowed to grow, over time they can eventually travel downward, poisoning the heart. Once this occurs, losing faith, even walking away, is possible, maybe inevitable. If only somewhere between the mind and the heart there were some kind of release valve … Wait! There is. We call this valve the mouth. If we stop the thoughts there and allow them to come out and be met with encouragement and truth, healing and health can occur. Then what our hearts may produce through our mouths is actually praise for the reality of the One we doubted!

Job struggled with the position in which God had allowed him to be placed, and he certainly, and understandably, complained. But look at his final message after God called him out.

> "No one can oppose you, because you have the power to do what you want. You asked why I talk so much when I know so little. I have talked about things that are far beyond my understanding. You told me to listen and answer your questions. I heard about you from others; now I have seen you with my own eyes." (Job 42:1–5 CEV)

Just like Job, Amy needs to see God with her own eyes. The only way for this to happen is through honest, open dialogue and transparency with the Creator—and the community of believers He has placed around her.

Remember: divert your doubts from reaching your heart by speaking them through your mouth so they become *deeper faith*, not *desperate fears*.

In your journal, take a few prayerful moments to write out your doubts and fears about your faith. God already knows exactly how you feel, so be honest and get them out onto the paper. Then, talk to God, and open up about them.

OPPOSITION OFFERS OPPORTUNITY

Grace is eating lunch alone in the teacher's lounge. Principal Kinney, a striking yet stern professional woman, enters. "Grace, I need to speak to you immediately."

Walking briskly down the hall, confused by the sudden crisis, Grace asks, "How did we get here so quickly? We're talking about something I said in class less than an hour ago!"

Kinney responds, "One of your students … don't ask who … sent a text to their parents, and it's already blowing up. I just need to hear it from you. Did this actually happen?"

Grace, gathering her composure, states, "If you're asking whether I responded to a student's question, the answer is yes. If you're asking whether her question—and my answer—both involved the teachings of Jesus within the context of my lesson, I'd also have to say yes."

At the end of the hall, Principal Kinney opens the double doors and motions for Grace to walk through, as she, now growing curt in her speech, snaps, "Grace, you have no idea how serious this is."

Ms. Rizzo, a fellow teacher and tenured veteran near retirement, is the school's union representative. She sits on one side of the table beside Grace, with Principal Kinney, the superintendant, and an attorney on the other side.

The superintendant begins, "I've asked Bob Fessler, the school's attorney, to sit in. He's here to advise us on any legal issues we might be up against."

Grace asks, "Should I have a lawyer too?"

"I don't think there's any need for that," the superintendent continues. "Ms. Rizzo is present as your representative. We're here to hear your side of the story, Ms. Wesley. I understand a student in your second-period history class asked a question about parallels between the teachings of Gandhi and remarks allegedly made by Jesus?"

Grace responds, "That's correct."

"And your answer incorporated specific, detailed reference to those teachings to include Scripture itself? The words of … Jesus?"

"Yes."

Ms. Rizzo leans in slightly and grits out, "What were you thinking, Grace?" Before she can respond, the inquisition marches on.

"And you believe your response was in line with district policy?"

"Yes."

The school's attorney chimes in. "As well as in conformity with state and federal guidelines?"

Grace, growing frustrated, responds yet again, "Yes."

The attorney, now looking grim, states, "Ms. Wesley, unfortunately for you, I'm fairly certain the board will disagree."

Grace starts to feel, from the attitude and tone in the room, that the school and her coworkers are distancing themselves from her.

———.———

Jesus was speaking with a few of His disciples when He began to prophesy:

"You will be handed over to the local councils and beaten in the synagogues. You will stand trial before governors and kings because you are my followers. But this will be your opportunity to tell them about me. For the Good News must first be preached to all nations. But when you are arrested and stand trial, don't worry in advance about what to say. Just say what God tells you at that time, for it is not you who will be speaking, but the Holy Spirit. … And everyone will hate you because you are my followers. But the one who endures to the end will be saved." (Mark 13:9–11, 13 NLT)

Today we are beginning to see lawsuits and jail time popping up for believers who will not back down. This has been happening for many years in foreign countries, but as the gospel begins to be silenced in our Western culture, the persecution now begins.

What does standing up for your faith look like for you? What does speaking up sound like in your circles? Where in your world is there opposition to Scripture? Who would distance themselves from you if you stood up for your faith? Who would encourage and affirm you?

Take a few moments and write your answers to the above questions in your journal. You may not feel these are reality at the moment, but like Grace, you could find yourself quickly in the middle of a storm, simply by being true to who—and whose—you are.

LISTEN UP!

Principal Kinney is at her desk on the phone, ready to put an end to the conversation. "Coach, I'm not sure you're hearing me. I said no prayers. No moments of silence. Nothing. Not on the field, in the locker room, or in the parking lot for that matter. Got it?" As she stabs the end-call button on her phone, she looks up to see Brooke standing in the doorway. There is an awkward moment, as she would have preferred the end of that one-way conversation not to have been overheard by a student.

"Hi, Brooke," Kinney says, quickly changing tones.

"You wanted to see me?" Brooke sits down across from the principal's desk.

Kinney switches back into all-business mode. "Ms. Wesley is currently under disciplinary review. All her classes have been reassigned, and until things are settled, I don't want you having *any* contact with her. None whatsoever—on or off school property."

Brooke, hurt and confused, responds, "Do I have any say in this?"

"No. I've already spoken with your father and he agrees with me."

Quietly, almost to herself, Brooke says, "Since when does my dad care?"

Kinney tries to reassure her. "The important thing to remember is you haven't done anything wrong."

Brooke now takes a stronger tone. "Neither did Ms. Wesley. All she did was answer a question."

"I believe Ms. Wesley's answer to your question was inappropriate."

Brooke, growing tired of the level of control everyone else is taking in her life, finds her voice. "Really? I mean, aren't we allowed to say what we believe? When did that change?"

———·———

Freedom of speech has never been at a more precarious crossroads than today. People have more outlets than ever to express their opinions—even anonymously on social media. Meanness and cowardice seem to be at an all-time high. But, at the same time, Christians are becoming more and more restricted due to the growing perception of statements of faith being "offensive."

The best regulator of our mouths is the Holy Spirit. He can tell us to speak when everyone else says to be quiet. He can also tell us to be silent when everyone expects us to speak.

Here are three thoughts for this ongoing battle in us all:

1. Listen more.
This is not about simply hearing, but proactively zeroing in on others' words, feelings, and thoughts. Active listening is a skill that we must constantly hone. We never arrive. For introverts, this means taking in what is being said to form the best

response. For extroverts, this means speaking less and listening more.

2. Make your words count.

Don't count your words, but make them count. When you speak—cut the chatter and make it matter. Wise people are not necessarily quiet people, but they listen, then say the right thing at the right time in the right way.

Isn't it ironic how "I'm sorry, I shouldn't have said that," and "I'm sorry, I should have said something" can have equal weight in offense in our relationships?

3. Ask Jesus for His ears and mouth.

While we certainly need all of Jesus in our communication, hearing people as He would and speaking to them the way He wants makes all the difference in how we understand others and how we are understood.

Whether speaking or listening, in everyday conversation or in critical situations, we can change our communication for the better. Christ can be Lord over our personalities, our ears, and our mouths. He knows exactly when to speak and when to listen.

> Everything in me will celebrate *when you speak what is right*. (Proverbs 23:16 NLT)

In your journal, complete these open-ended sentences:

The situation where I most feel I can't speak my mind is …

The situation where I feel I usually say too much is …

The place I most want to allow the Holy Spirit to speak through me is …

THE LAST WORD

Walking into her usual coffee shop, Grace grabs her cell phone and punches in the digits on the business card. A man in his midthirties spots her and walks over. Meet Tom Endler, a rather unconventional lawyer. He's handsome with a stubble beard, casual dress, and well-worn shoes.

"Grace? Are you Grace?"

She nods.

"I'm your union-appointed attorney," Tom says.

Grace shakes his hand, now looking skeptical. "You don't really look like a lawyer."

He smiles. "Thank you."

She tries to course correct. "I'm not sure I meant it as a compliment."

"But I'm determined to take it as one," he quips back with a grin.

Knowing she has little choice, she asks, "Have you defended many teachers in disciplinary matters?"

"Nope," he says. "You'll be my first. I was just hired on from the public defender's office."

Surprised, Grace says, "Criminal law? No offense, but I'm not a criminal."

"Don't be too sure of that," the attorney states. "Your kind of case makes everybody uncomfortable—school board, teachers, and parents.

"Grace, I'm going to level with you. Nobody wants your case. I drew it because I'm the low man in a place where seniority means everything. If, for whatever reason, you don't approve of me, then you'll be on your own. You're free to hire your own attorney—out of your own pocket—but educational law isn't exactly a common specialty."

She is taken aback by his candor. "Is there any good news?"

Tom is ready for this question too. "I don't like to lose … and I'm willing to fight for you."

"Are you a believer?" she asks.

The lawyer in him comes out. "You mean a Christian? No. But I think that's an advantage for you."

"Why?" Grace asks.

"Because you're passionate about what you believe, and let's face it, it's why you're in trouble in the first place. But it blinds you to the realities of procedure."

Grace returns to her confident tone. "Okay, I agree for you to represent me."

———·———

Peter and John had been brought before the council of Jewish elders and teachers of the law for preaching publicly about Jesus. After questioning the two, the council threatened them but let them go in fear of a riot among the people. Their release greatly encouraged all the believers in seeing God's protection and sovereignty at work on their behalf.

When they heard the report, all the believers lifted their voices together in prayer to God: "O Sovereign Lord, Creator of heaven and earth, the sea, and everything in them—you spoke long ago by the Holy Spirit through our ancestor David, your servant, saying, 'Why were the nations so angry? Why did they waste their time with futile plans? The kings of the earth prepared for battle; the rulers gathered together against the LORD and against his Messiah.' In fact, this has happened here in this very city! For Herod Antipas, Pontius Pilate the governor, the Gentiles, and the people of Israel were all united against Jesus, your holy servant, whom you anointed. But everything they did was determined beforehand according to your will." (Acts 4:24–28 NLT)

A common theme throughout Scripture is that no matter how the circumstances may appear, man never has the last word—God does.

King Nebuchadnezzar may have thought he was throwing Shadrach, Meshach, and Abednego to their fiery death, but God had another plan.

King Darius may have thought he was sending Daniel to death in the lions' den, but God had another plan.

King Saul may have thought he could get rid of David forever, but God had another plan.

Governor Pilate may have thought he was getting rid of Jesus, but God had another plan.

Do you see the pattern? God always, always, always has the last word.

In your journal, complete these three open-ended sentences:

With the situation I am the most worried about today, the worst thing that could happen is …

If the worst thing does happen, then the way God could have a different or a better plan is to …

In all my worries and concerns today, God could have the final word by …

THE VALLEY VARIABLE

G race is sitting in the quiet of her bedroom floor, her Bible open in front of her. Her heart and soul are in turmoil over the circumstances in which she finds herself.

She begins to read out loud, "Trust in the Lord with all your heart and lean not on your own understanding. In all your ways, acknowledge Him and He will make your paths straight." She pauses, letting the words not only comfort her, but provide her with the strength for what she must do.

She prays aloud, "Father, I need You. I can't do this alone. I know that You are in control. Please give me the courage I need. In Jesus' name. Amen." Her fear begins to subside as she feels a familiar strength begin to flood her spirit.

———·———

In 1 Kings 20, we find Syria planning to attack Israel again. The Syrian leaders make this decision: Last time, Israel defeated us in the hills, so that's the reason we lost. If we can fight them on flat land, in the valley between the mountains, we can win.

The following spring he called up the Aramean army and marched out against Israel, this time at Aphek.

Israel then mustered its army, set up supply lines, and marched out for battle. But the Israelite army looked like two little flocks of goats in comparison to the vast Aramean forces that filled the countryside!

Then the man of God went to the king of Israel and said, "This is what the LORD says: The Arameans have said, 'The LORD is a god of the hills and not of the plains.' So I will defeat this vast army for you. Then you will know that I am the LORD." (1 Kings 20:26–28 NLT)

Just a few verses further, we see God prove He is Lord over not only the hills but the valleys as well.

We can read a passage like this and think, *How ridiculous! Why would they excuse their defeat by thinking God is limited to certain areas? Why would they blame location?*

Here's how we often create this same scenario in our own lives…

I believe He is God over my family, but I can't trust Him with my finances.

I believe He is God over my church, but not my career.

I believe He will watch over my kids, but He can't change my marriage.

I believe He is God over forgiveness of sin, but not the healing of my heart.

I believe He can intervene in a crisis, but not in the little details of my life.

I believe He blesses everyone I know—but not me.

Do you see the God-of-the-hills-but-not-the-valleys syndrome that we can also create? The limitations we place on a limitless God? The way we apply faith in one area and not another?

So, for you, where are your hills where God rules? But where are your valleys where you believe He doesn't—or can't? What will it take for Him to be Lord over your entire life— every hill and every valley?

For Grace, she has known God to be the Lord of her family, her teaching career, and her relationships, but He is now taking her to a deeper valley where she has never traveled. He's asking her to go alone—with only Him. With God's track record, these seasons usually lead to not just hills, but mountains, except with an entirely new perspective, crafted in the valley.

Faith is a journey, not a destination, so, for today, why not just let Him take over the next valley in your life?

> I look up to the mountains—does my help come from there? My help comes from the LORD, who made heaven and earth! (Psalm 121:1–2 NLT)

In your journal, write down a valley you are in right now where you struggle to believe God could win for you. Next, write down a mountain you were able to reach through the hand of God. Consider any place you are limiting God because of your perspective of His location. During your prayer time, talk to Him about your faith and your doubts. Look to the mountain!

GETTIN' OUT OF THE GRAY

Grace and Tom sit down on one side of the large conference table. On the other side, the superintendant, the school attorney, and Principal Kinney sit with what feels like a small army. Grace can quickly see the union designed to *protect* her is now about protecting itself *from* her.

The superintendant wastes no time cutting to the chase. "Call to order! I assume Ms. Wesley knows this board has the power to recommend any number of disciplinary actions, up to and including her termination?"

Just as Grace leans forward to speak, Tom jumps in. "She does. And the board should be aware that in the event of such termination, which we would view as both wrongful and without cause, she reserves all rights of redress."

Suddenly, the intensity in the room grows. The school's attorney says, "There might be a way around this unpleasantness that would satisfy all parties. A disciplinary notice in Ms. Wesley's file stating the board's objections to her behavior, as well as a response from Ms. Wesley confessing the inappropriateness of her actions and an apology, along with a pledge *not* to engage in similar discussion regarding Jesus in the future."

With this "olive branch," Tom feels like he is about to wrap this case up. "I'm confident we can move forward on that basis—"

"No. I can't," Grace interrupts.

Tom immediately asks the committee for a word in the hallway with his client. In a half whisper, half shout, he tells Grace, "This is the part where you say you're sorry, thank me as your lawyer, then go back to your classroom, pick up your life, and move on."

Grace digs deep. "But I can't do that."

Tom, not yet comprehending the level of her convictions, asks why.

"Because in my class, I gave an honest answer to a legitimate question in a setting where I'm responsible for speaking the facts," she declares.

"Grace, you don't want to do this. It's the wrong decision," he responds, his frustration turning to desperation.

"Is it? I'd rather stand with God and be judged by the world than stand with the world and be judged by God. I am not going to be afraid to say the name of Jesus."

———·———

The writings of the New Testament are perfectly clear on announcing or renouncing Christ. There is no gray area found in Scripture.

> "I tell you, whoever publicly acknowledges me before others, the Son of Man will also acknowledge before the angels of God. But whoever disowns me before others will be disowned before the angels of God." (Luke 12:8–9 NIV)

Consider these two simple points:

1. Speak up

As was often the case, Jesus made this very simple: You acknowledge me before people, I acknowledge you. You deny me before people, I deny you. We must speak up about our relationship with Him and make our faith public.

While this statement may sound harsh on the surface, God has already acknowledged us all by declaring anyone can be saved through the work of redemption on the cross. So now He waits for our response. If we accept the relationship and announce His presence in our lives, the covenant with Him is forever sealed.

Jesus is not a secret—He's a Savior!

2. Step up

Titus 1:16 states, "They claim to know God, but by their actions they deny him" (NIV). This verse states in no uncertain terms that just saying we know God and not backing it up with actions is worthless. Our actions are always an outward expression of our hearts. One of the worst indictments for a believer is for someone to say, "Wow, really? He's a Christian? I had no idea."

If God is indeed alive in your life, people need to know. Speak up and step up!

In your journal today, complete these sentences:

One place I know I need to speak up is …

One place I know I need to step up is …

One place I have spoken up is …

One place I have stepped up is …

THE END OF THE STORY

While Tom and Grace are out in the hall, Principal Kinney says, "She's not gonna go for it. I know her. Two thousand years ago, she'd be in the arena, trying to make friends with the lions."

The superintendant looks to the lawyer. "How do we make this go away and not get blood on our hands?"

"We let a civil liberties organization do it for us," the attorney says. "They file suit against Ms. Wesley, and if she's found liable—which she will be—then we fire her for cause."

The superintendant voices concern. "But the school district will surely be named as a codefendant. We don't have the financial wherewithal to—"

The attorney interjects, "They've already been in touch, and they aren't interested in punishing the school. They … want … her."

Kinney, in full protection mode, asks, "Are you sure?"

The attorney smiles. "Trust me. They've been dreaming of a case like this."

After Tom and Grace come back into the meeting, Tom, who can't believe he is reading what feels like his own death warrant, says, "While Ms. Wesley apologizes for any inconvenience her actions may have caused, Ms. Wesley stands by her statements and does not retract or recant them either in full or in part."

Following protocol, the superintendant responds, "So noted. Having little choice, this board recommends continued suspension—henceforth without pay—pending further review by a court of competent jurisdiction, to determine whether or not Ms. Wesley violated local, state, or federal guidelines. *This* proceeding is adjourned."

Though filled with concern and uncertainty, deep down, Grace knows she is doing the right thing, and more importantly, honoring God with her life, words, and actions.

———·———

Unfortunately, we live in a day where many are volatile and hostile toward God's truth and standards. There has always been and always will be this brand of people throughout history and in every culture. Principal Kinney made a reference to Grace and the lions that the early Christians faced, which reminds us of a story…

King Darius had promoted Daniel to the very top of the government due to his high values, wisdom, and excellence. But the other leaders didn't like Daniel's standards. So they decided to use them against him.

Daniel was known to pray three times a day with his windows open toward his home of Jerusalem.

So the administrators and high officers went to the king and said, "Long live King Darius! We are all in agreement—we administrators, officials, high officers, advisers, and governors—that the king should make a law that will be strictly enforced. Give orders that for the next thirty days any person who prays to anyone, divine or human—except to you, Your Majesty—will be thrown into the den of lions. And now, Your Majesty, issue and sign this law so it cannot be changed, an official law of the Medes and Persians that cannot be revoked." So King Darius signed the law. (Daniel 6:6–9 NLT)

Does this sound at all familiar to the school attorney's line: "Trust me. They've been dreaming of a case like this"?

Daniel's story went like this:

As always, he prayed.

The officers tattled on him.

The king was forced to uphold his own law, even under the trickery of his leaders.

Daniel was thrown into the lion's den.

God saved him, and the king saw the hand of God at work through Daniel.

The king threw the officers—and their families—to the lions.

The king publicly recognized God, and Daniel continued to prosper.

Now, here's a question: What if you stopped reading Daniel's story when the king threw him into the den? What might you assume?

Today, things look bad for Grace, don't they? It looks like standing up for God and holding your ground ends badly. But her story is not over yet, just like Daniel's wasn't finished in the lion's den.

Inviting Christ into the middle of your crisis can change

everything. The story is not over until He says it is over. Because God is indeed alive!

In your journal, write down your worst crisis and then write out what you would like to see God do by "the end of the story." Then write out a prayer asking Him to bring about *His* ending in *His* time.

TURNING THE TABLES

Peter Kane is a Harvard-educated, seasoned, hard-charging lawyer with chiseled good looks and a trail of expendable people lying in his wake. Tonight, he sits in Richard and Catherine Thawley's living room, discussing the case involving Brooke and Grace. Kane has smelled an irresistible opportunity for a one-two punch of silencing Christians *and* making money.

Catherine states, "The last thing we need is a bunch of religious fanatics protesting outside our house."

Kane assures, "We'll work to keep it out of the media … for now. And next year, every college application can tell the story of how Brooke was part of a landmark constitutional case concerning separation of church and state. There's not an Ivy League admissions board that can resist that." The thought sells Catherine on the idea. He continues, "Think of all the other innocent children out there who've been subjected to their repressive belief system. And let's not forget the financial opportunity here."

Brooke has been standing on the other side of the wall, listening to their conversation, as she hears the hotshot lawyer say, "Ms. Wesley is a school board employee, and a win here clearly establishes misconduct by their paid employee. Nothing changes policy faster than an expensive settlement. We are going to prove once and for all that God is dead."

Clearly understanding their real agenda, Brooke comes around the corner, choosing to enter the room at that exact moment. She stares at them all with disgust, then she storms out of the room.

———·———

Part of the Enemy's plan to silence and destroy God's people has always seemed to be about singling out a few to make an example for everyone to see. Fear and intimidation have always been a strong suit of the opposition to the kingdom.

In the book of Esther, we find Haman, the highest of all the nobles in Persia. He became jealous of, and enraged by, the integrity and character of Mordecai, a Jewish man whose cousin was Queen Esther. So Haman devised a plan to not only wipe out Mordecai but all of the Jewish people. But King Xerxes and Mordecai had a history—the Jew had once uncovered a plot to kill the king and saved him.

When Queen Esther shared Haman's plot with the king, he ordered him to be hanged on the very gallows that Haman had intended for Mordecai. Esther then pleaded with the king to stop Haman's orders for the execution of her people.

> Then Mordecai left the king's presence, wearing the royal robe of blue and white, the great crown of gold, and an outer cloak of fine linen and purple. And the

people of Susa celebrated the new decree. The Jews were filled with joy and gladness and were honored everywhere. In every province and city, wherever the king's decree arrived, the Jews rejoiced and had a great celebration and declared a public festival and holiday. And many of the people of the land became Jews themselves, for they feared what the Jews might do to them. (Esther 8:15–17 NLT)

A quite similar event happened when Satan thought he had finally done away with Jesus. The Christ was crucified and buried. The healing, deliverance, and miracles were over—or so he thought. On the third day, everything changed. The plan didn't work, because God's power will always be stronger than any force of evil in this world.

Do you believe God's plan for your life can prevail over the enemy? Do you trust that there is a "third day" coming in your life, where you will see the Lord's victory?

No matter what tongues accuse you, what rulers come against you, or what weapon is aimed at you, God is bigger, stronger, and faster than anything that can oppose you. Believe this today as the truth in your life. Thank God He includes you in His plan, protection, and power.

In your journal, list out the enemy's plans you feel are plotting against you right now. Next, write out the accusations anyone may be leveling at you. Finally, hand your lists over to God and ask Him to handle the "Hamans" in your life. Then trust Him to take care of you.

FAIRNESS AND FAVOR

Tom and Grace are sitting at her kitchen table, going over the case. Grace, looking over some papers, asks, "Injunctive relief?"

Tom tries to explain. "They're asking that you be fired, plus revocation of your teaching certificate, plus attorney's fees. Essentially, you'll lose everything."

She tries to wrap her head around his words. "Why are they doing this?"

"They want to make an example of you. To them, your beliefs are like a disease whose time has come and gone. Sort of like smallpox, polio, or the plague."

"So what do we do?" she asks in disbelief and desperation.

He looks her in the eye and answers, "We win."

———·———

One of the most obvious questions Grace would have to ask, especially as a Christian, is, "Why me? What did I ever do to deserve this?"

One of the most unfortunate truths we all must learn as soon as possible as we navigate the storms of this world is,

"Life is not fair." Sin forever sealed this saying into our very existence. When we study harder than anyone in the class and still fail the test, we realize life is not fair. When we work harder than anyone in the place and the promotion goes to the boss' favorite, life is not fair. When someone you feel like you can't live without suddenly leaves or dies, life is not fair. Daily, we are reminded of this difficult truth. Bad things don't just happen to good people, but to everyone.

An amazing example of living for Christ amidst constant unfair circumstances was the apostle Paul. Who would have blamed him for praying, *Lord, as soon as you get me out of this prison for speaking in Your name, I'll get back to ministry and writing letters to all the churches*? But he never waited on *man's fairness*, because he only cared about *God's favor*, which was always present—whether in a prison or a palace.

> "And now I am bound by the Spirit to go to Jerusalem. I don't know what awaits me, except that the Holy Spirit tells me in city after city that jail and suffering lie ahead. But my life is worth nothing to me unless I use it for finishing the work assigned me by the Lord Jesus—the work of telling others the Good News about the wonderful grace of God." (Acts 20:22–24 NLT)

Tom looked at Grace and communicated to her that he was fully focused—not on her feelings—but on fighting to win her case. Paul told his fellow believers he was committed to working for the King of Kings, regardless of what may be brought his way.

God might never ask you to go to trial over His name, much less be put into prison like Paul. But one thing is for certain—your life is about "finishing the work assigned to you by the Lord Jesus—the work of telling others the Good News about the wonderful grace of God." He knows exactly what this means in your life because He created you and has equipped you for this purpose.

Do you know your calling in Christ? Others may give counsel, but your life's work and ministry is personal between you and your heavenly Father. Go to Him to find out. With man, life will never be fair, but you can trust that you can live in God's favor, no matter what comes your way.

In your journal, write down one situation happening in your life right now that you feel is not fair. Next, write down a circumstance where you sense God's favor on you. Lastly, write down what you believe to be the work God has given you for your life's calling. Close by praying for your first situation, thanking Him for the second, and committing to Him today for the third.

THE FAITH FILTER

The day arrives for Grace's jury selection, and guess who we find is a potential juror? Our very own Pastor Dave. As the reverend is called up, Kane, the civil liberties lawyer, states, "Your Honor, we'd like to challenge for cause."

Stately and no-nonsense Presiding Judge Robert Stennis asks, "Why is that?"

"Your Honor, he's an ordained minister. Need I say more?"

Stennis nods. "The juror is excused."

Dave thinks to himself, *I knew they would get rid of me quick.*

"Objection, Your Honor!" Tom calls out.

"What basis, Mr. Endler?" the judge asks.

"Discriminatory, Your Honor. Peremptory challenges cannot be used to discriminate against a certain class of jurors by race, ethnic background, religion, or gender. The fact that religious belief is tangential to this case doesn't change that. Mr. Kane's insistence that this isn't about faith means the juror's personal belief should be a nonissue."

Stennis agrees. "Upon further reflection, I find the respondent's assertion is correct. Sustained." The judge looks at Dave and asks, "You're not her pastor, are you?" referring to Grace.

Pastor Dave, now a bit in shock, answers, "No, Your Honor."

Kane is also shocked. "Your Honor! I must protest!"

"Mr. Kane," Stennis firmly announces, "I have already ruled on this juror's eligibility. You had a set number of peremptory challenges—all of which you have used. Therefore it's up to opposing counsel."

Tom, glad for the small victory, states, "We accept him, Your Honor."

Dave mutters under his breath, "Better chance of being struck by lightning."

—·—

But the Lord said to Samuel, "Do not consider his appearance or his height, for I have rejected him. The Lord does not look at the things people look at. People look at the outward appearance, but the Lord looks at the heart."

Jesse had seven of his sons pass before Samuel, but Samuel said to him, "The Lord has not chosen these." So he asked Jesse, "Are these all the sons you have?" "There is still the youngest," Jesse answered. "He is tending the sheep." Samuel said, "Send for him; we will not sit down until he arrives." So he sent for him and had him brought in. He was glowing with health and had a fine appearance and handsome features. Then the Lord said, "Rise and anoint him; this is the one." So Samuel took the horn of oil and anointed him in the presence of his brothers, and from that day on

the Spirit of the LORD came powerfully upon David.
(1 Samuel 16:7, 10–13 NIV)

The spiritual aspect of life creates an entirely new outlook on everything—from the jurors picked in what seems like a hopeless trial to the choosing of a nation's king. But how can we learn to view life from God's perspective?

A professional photographer has various lenses and filters to achieve certain shots and angles to capture a moment. If we evaluate our view of the world, we will quickly see how we apply our own "lenses and filters" to life, depending on the person, situation, and even our own attitude at the time.

For one person, we may put on a skeptical, cautious filter. For another, a positive lens is applied through which we see even the negative. For someone else, we use a wide-angle lens to keep some distance. Honestly, attaching and detaching lenses and filters on our communication can be exhausting.

Viewing life as God does requires a prayerful application—throw away all the lenses and filters, applying only one—the Holy Spirit. He is able to adjust to every person, conversation, and setting to get exactly the right perspective to deal with anything and everyone in our lives. He knows how to properly capture every moment and make the right choice—even if it looks ridiculous to the world—to look straight at the heart.

In your journal, take a moment to evaluate and write down your own set of lenses and filters for relationships. Next, write down a few people or situations where you should ask the Lord to give you His filter to make the best choice. Where do you need "the Spirit of the Lord to come in power"?

MOVING MOUNTAINS

Pastor Dave comes out of his office into the sanctuary and sees Martin, who has quickly become a regular fixture around the church since coming to faith in Christ. The reverend calls out, "Hey, Martin. How's it going?"

Martin smiles. "Very good, Pastor Dave."

"Are you sure? What's going on?" Dave asks, knowing Martin is constantly contemplating a new and deep spiritual concept.

Martin begins, "Well, it seems like for every question you answer for me, three or four more spring up."

Pastor Dave smiles knowingly. "Yeah, but that's a good thing. It's like what Einstein said about science—picture what you know like the light of a candle: 'As the circle of knowledge expands, so does the circumference of darkness around it.'" He makes a circling gesture with his hands.

Martin suddenly strikes his "oh, I get it now" look. "So I am actually learning, even though it might not feel like it!"

Pastor Dave smiles again, "Exactly. So what's your next question?"

Martin immediately launches into another thought. "Well,

I've been studying the Beatitudes. They are very hard—one might say impossible—to follow completely. Here in Luke's account, Jesus says: 'Do unto others as you would have them do unto you,' but how is this possible? How can I react to everyone else's needs as I would to my own—even for one day, let alone my whole life? And how am I supposed to reconcile my inability to do so with this Scripture?"

Reverend Dave grins. "Yeah. That's a good one. Okay, scoot over, Martin. Now let's take a look at that chapter."

———

Martin would have fit in quite well with the deep religious questions the Jewish people had in Jesus' day. While there are countless interpretations regarding the Sermon on the Mount, here is one very simple and practical version, using a mountain as a visual image.

"Blessed are the poor in spirit, for theirs is the kingdom of heaven" (Matthew 5:3 NIV).

Poor in spirit means a bankrupt state in our souls. We have nothing in and of ourselves to pay our debt of sin. Therefore, we are in great need.

"Blessed are those who mourn, for they will be comforted" (Matthew 5:4 NIV).

Realizing there is no way to meet our need, we now mourn our state of being because of the destitute condition of our hearts.

"Blessed are the meek, for they will inherit the earth" (Matthew 5:5 NIV).

Meekness comes out of humility as a result of understanding our need and our sin.

"Blessed are those who hunger and thirst for righteousness, for they will be filled" (Matthew 5:6 NIV).

Because of this state we are in, we hunger and thirst for something greater than, above, and outside ourselves.

"Blessed are the merciful, for they will be shown mercy" (Matthew 5:7 NIV).

Then comes God's provision to meet our needs. He fills us and we are blessed and fully satisfied. We then become merciful for we have been shown great mercy.

"Blessed are the pure in heart, for they will see God" (Matthew 5:8 NIV).

The mercy we receive brings purity to the heart, allowing us to see, hear, and sense the presence of God.

"Blessed are the peacemakers, for they will be called children of God" (Matthew 5:9 NIV).

And, finally, we become advocates, ambassadors, and peacemakers for God as we now understand and submit to a relationship with Him.

We came out of the valley and up the mountain in verses 3, 4, and 5, crested the summit in verse 6, then came down the other side as a new person in 7, 8, and 9.

When you realize you are poor in spirit, totally dependent on God, you then become merciful to others.

When you mourn over the impure state of your heart, then and only then can your heart be cleansed and purified by God's power.

Meekness reigns in the heart and life of a peacemaker.

In your journal, draw a mountain or a "bell curve" and graph your life with God. Reread each of the seven verses and evaluate your growth in each area. Close with a prayer, asking God for more of His kingdom, comfort, meekness, righteousness, mercy, purity, and peace.

FAME IN THE NAME

I t's day one at Grace's trial, and prosecuting attorney Kane begins his opening remarks to the jury.

"The plaintiffs I represent are the aggrieved parents of a student in Ms. Wesley's class who was subjected to hearing the teachings of Jesus Christ being favorably compared to those of Mahatma Gandhi—as though they were both equally true. Gandhi says this and Jesus says that. But to parents who are trying to raise their daughter to be a freethinker, outside any established religious tradition, this was highly offensive. We all know that Jesus belongs to one particular religious tradition. And by reciting the words alleged to be attributable to this religious figure, who allegedly existed some two thousand years ago, not to mention Ms. Wesley's rote memorization of not only the words of Scripture but the exact citation of them, constitutes a clear and compelling indication of what she believes, what she supports, and what she endorses. Preaching, not teaching. That's what Ms. Wesley did.

"So why are we here today? Because Ms. Wesley refused to apologize. If it wasn't her intention to breach the Establishment Clause—the separation of church and state—she would've taken the opportunity afforded to her by the school district to apologize—but she didn't. And this shows that her true motivation was to turn an innocent question into an opportunity to preach.

"If we grant Ms. Wesley the right to violate the law based solely on private beliefs, our society will collapse. I implore you, as part of your sworn duty to our country, please do not set this precedent. The future of our republic depends on it."

———·———

Have you ever wondered why the name of Jesus is so controversial and can create so much trouble? Well, when was the last time you heard someone hit their thumb with a hammer and yell, "Buddha!" Or become frustrated with someone and exclaim, "Hare Krishna! What were you thinking?!" While there are countless prophets and religious leaders throughout history—real and fictional—culturally we have come to accept and validate the inherent power and authority in Jesus' name.

Grace's trial wasn't over the use of Gandhi's name. That seemed to be no big deal to anyone. This "offense" and uproar was about speaking the name of Jesus.

The reason His name is used in the many ways and forms it is and why it is so controversial is this: there is actual power in Jesus' name.

When he appeared in human form, he humbled himself in obedience to God and died a criminal's death on a cross. Therefore, God elevated him to the place of highest honor and gave him the name above all other names, that at the name of Jesus every knee should bow, in heaven and on earth and under the earth, and every tongue declare that Jesus Christ is Lord to the glory of God the Father. (Philippians 2:7–11 NLT)

Grace's trial is not actually about separation of church and state, religious rights, or legal precedent, but about one thing and one thing only: Jesus—His name, authority, and power. If He were truly an "alleged" person, then why fight so hard against Him? This is exactly what we saw between Professor Radisson and Josh. And, in the end, the energy expended to prove God is dead was only about someone's very raw and real need for healing—healing needed from the very One whom all the fuss was about.

Today's passage tells us, in the end, *every* knee will bow and *every* tongue will confess. On that day, the glory of God will reveal Him to all mankind. No one will be forced to bow. They will fully realize who He is.

Isn't it ironic that what *Grace* is accused of doing is exactly what *everyone* will do on the final day?

In your journal, write down a situation where you saw Jesus' name cause a controversy. Next, write down a situation that desperately needed His name for healing and hope. Is there any place in your life where you are shying away from using Jesus' name? Is there a place in your life right now where you desperately need Jesus' power to come through for you? Connect the dots. Maybe speaking His name more will make more room for His power in your life.

LORD OF LIBERTY

N ow, it is Tom's turn in the courtroom. He begins, "Ladies and gentlemen of the jury: I have, here in my hands, a copy of the Constitution of the United States of America and the Bill of Rights—arguably, the two most important documents in the history of our great nation. Within these are contained a list of our rights and duties, our freedoms and obligations as citizens. But despite Mr. Kane's impassioned rhetoric, you know what you *won't* find in here, no matter how hard you look? The phrase 'separation of church and state.' That's right. It's not there and it never has been. Because that phrase comes from a letter written by Thomas Jefferson, which, ironically, he was writing to a Baptist congregation, assuring them that they would always have the right to believe as they wished—free of government interference.

"But lately, that phrase—taken out of context—has often been twisted and contorted to mean exactly the opposite, as Mr. Kane is looking to do. I hope you understand that my client has rights, rights that trump his agenda."

———·———

Beliefs taken out of context. Twisted. Contorted. Convictions removed. We see these at play every day in our world. But this is nothing new.

> Later, Matthew invited Jesus and his disciples to his home as dinner guests, along with many tax collectors and other disreputable sinners. But when the Pharisees saw this, they asked his disciples, "Why does your teacher eat with such scum?" (Matthew 9:10–11 NLT)

> But the Pharisees said, "He can cast out demons because he is empowered by the prince of demons." (Matthew 9:34 NLT)

> Then Jesus went over to their synagogue, where he noticed a man with a deformed hand. The Pharisees asked Jesus, "Does the law permit a person to work by healing on the Sabbath?" (They were hoping he would say yes, so they could bring charges against him.) (Matthew 12:9–10 NLT)

Do you see the pattern here? These men who were the teachers of the Law placed their own version and interpretation over anything else—even over healing a man's deformity. Today, there are many who want to open up "rights" to any and everyone while silencing and bullying Christians into obscurity.

We are all capable of being legalists, of putting the rules and law before the hearts of people. To avoid the pitfalls of this ungodly and self-centered mind-set, here are a few helpful ideas.

1. Stay teachable.

When we're young, we can't wait to become adults, so "no one can tell us what to do." But the truth is we must remain moldable and teachable to stay in God's will. No matter our age or experience, He has much to teach us, sometimes from the most unexpected places.

The Pharisees believed they knew everything and were above anyone. We must stay clear of this attitude and stay close to Jesus.

2. Stay grace-focused.

While we must certainly keep man's laws and God's laws, the grace of God should shape our decisions regarding others. If we constantly find ourselves criticizing and judging others based on their behavior and what we think they should do or not do, we can err on the side of the Law and not exhibit God's grace.

Allowing His grace to flow freely in your own life gives you the freedom to give grace to others.

3. Stay humble.

The reason people twist original truths such as "separation of church and state" is they stop looking to God as the Giver of Law and begin to place themselves as judge and jury. Humility before God and others will keep the main thing the main thing.

In your journal, write down any place you know you need to be more teachable, more grace focused, and more humble. Write down anywhere you may be leaning more toward a Pharisee's attitude and then consider how you can bring more of Jesus to that setting.

BREAKING DOWN BARRIERS

Today, we continue with Tom's opening statements to the jury.

"One morning, my client, Ms. Wesley, started her day as usual. She made breakfast for her dependent grandfather and drove to work at her job as a teacher at Martin Luther King Jr. High School, a place where she was voted Teacher of the Year.

"Her lesson plan for second-period AP History that morning didn't contain any mention of God, or Jesus, or any other faith-related terms. She didn't have a Bible on her desk in plain sight. She didn't write about Jesus on the board. She wasn't looking to preach or proselytize. She didn't start the class with a blessing or lead the students in prayer. No." Tom pauses for effect.

"All she did was answer a question. Honestly and to the best of her knowledge and ability. Because that's what she gets paid to do—answer questions. And for this, she's being made an example of.

"I find myself asking: Is this the America we want to live in? Mr. Kane will insist, loudly and often, that faith isn't on trial here. But that's *exactly* what's on trial. The most basic human right of all: the right to *believe*!

"Or are we now in the business of making people deny their faith? Mr. Kane thinks so. He and his staff have traveled a long way to be here today. Not one of them lives within a thousand miles of here. But they've come to make sure that they put a final nail in the coffin of faith in the public square. To insure that any question that even brushes up against faith can never be answered, except to say, 'We can't talk about that.'"

———·———

One evening in the cover of darkness, a Pharisee named Nicodemus, who may not have been that different from Attorney Kane, sought out Jesus. He began to ask many questions and was confused by Jesus' answers about being born again and the kingdom of God.

> "How are these things possible?" Nicodemus asked. Jesus replied, "You are a respected Jewish teacher, and yet you don't understand these things? I assure you, we tell you what we know and have seen, and yet you won't believe our testimony. But if you don't believe me when I tell you about earthly things, how can you possibly believe if I tell you about heavenly things?" (John 3:9–12 NLT)

As Jesus used analogies of water and the wind—things of the earth—referring to the Spirit, he saw Nicodemus struggle to comprehend His teaching. In essence, He was saying, *As respected, smart, and articulate as you are, if you can't get what*

I'm talking about at this level, there's no point in going deeper in my explanation.

Consider these barriers we can have to faith:

Intellect	Attitude	Past Experiences
Religiousness	Reputation	Titles
Emotional Baggage	Legalism	Pride
Personal Goals/Agendas		Wealth/Power

Barriers that people put up against faith and belief can become so deep and so high that they actually start to become offensive and not just defensive. Antifaith folks can begin to think, *Not only am I not going to believe—I don't want anyone else to either!*

Nicodemus was obviously being drawn by the Holy Spirit toward truth for him to risk his reputation and title by going to speak with Jesus—even in the dark of night. As we encounter the "Attorney Kanes" and the "Nicodemuses" in our lives, we can't be defensive or exhibit anger toward them, for such an approach only fuels their fire. We must always give them God's love along with His truth. They need to see Jesus, not "our point."

Take a look at the above list of barriers and ask yourself if any of these are present in your life. Take a moment to write down any thoughts you have or feel. Close by praying for your own barriers and also for any "Kane" or "Nicodemus" you have in your life.

PATIENT, PREPARED, AND PASSIONATE

Grace's trial is now moving forward, with witnesses being called to the stand. After Brooke's dad, Mr. Thawley, has been questioned and steps down from the stand, Kane then calls Ms. Rizzo, the teacher's union rep, to testify. He asks her, "Does Ms. Wesley talk about faith issues on the school campus?"

Rizzo responds, "All the time. Everyone knows she's a Christian. I don't think she'd chew a stick of gum without praying first. It makes everyone feel awkward." If Grace had any doubt how Rizzo felt about her, that question is now well answered.

Kane gives a slight, smug smile. "No further questions, Your Honor."

Judge Stennis looks at Tom. "Your witness, Mr. Endler."

He begins, "Ms. Rizzo, you stated that Ms. Wesley talks about faith 'all the time.' I'm curious. Can you give us a specific instance?" Rizzo looks a bit deer-caught-in-the-headlights by the question.

"No, not off the top of my head."

Tom continues, not surprised by the answer, "Hmm. Well,

has she, as far as you're aware, ever started her class with a prayer?"

"No," Rizzo answers.

"Ever asked anyone in the teacher's lounge to pray with her?"

"No," she answers—a bit quieter.

Tom keeps rolling. "Asked you personally to pray with her?"

Suddenly, Kane pipes up, "Objection, Your Honor! Cumulative. The question has effectively been asked and answered."

Tom interjects, "Your Honor, Ms. Rizzo's sworn testimony says that Ms. Wesley talked about her faith 'all the time.' Yet, she failed to cite a single instance. I'm merely trying to discover some basis for her opinion."

Judge Stennis says, "Sustained. Mr. Endler, we're done with this line of questioning."

Tom adjusts and asks, "Ms. Rizzo, in the school's initial inquiry into this matter, you were Ms. Wesley's representative on behalf of the teacher's union, were you not?"

Rizzo nods. "Yes."

Tom moves closer, asking, "And did you ever consider that your disapproval of Ms. Wesley's faith might taint your ability to represent her properly?"

Again, Kane stands and protests, "Objection! Speculative."

Again, Stennis sides with Kane. "Sustained."

At that moment, a juror sneezes. Instinctively, Pastor Dave says, "God bless you." Tom turns to Dave and says, "Careful … or you might end up on trial."

While most everyone laughs, they also know that concept can't be too far from the truth, simply because of why they are sitting in the courtroom at all!

———·———

What a great testimony for Grace's Christian walk that someone would say, essentially, that everyone knows she is a Christian and has the impression she speaks of her faith all the time, yet they can't recall any circumstances where she abused or overstepped her role as a professional. What an admirable balance.

> Who is going to harm you if you are eager to do good? But even if you should suffer for what is right, you are blessed. "Do not fear their threats; do not be frightened." But in your hearts revere Christ as Lord. Always be prepared to give an answer to everyone who asks you to give the reason for the hope that you have. But do this with gentleness and respect, keeping a clear conscience, so that those who speak maliciously against your good behavior in Christ may be ashamed of their slander. For it is better, if it is God's will, to suffer for doing good than for doing evil. (1 Peter 3:13–17 NIV)

Grace had accomplished her reputation by the exact things we see in these verses. Here are a few takeaways from this passage:

1. When we work for good, we always win, even if life makes it look like we are temporarily losing.

2. When we do what is right, we don't need to fear the future.

3. Staying ready to speak for Christ gives us the right words when the questions come.

4. Walking in gentleness and respect brings a clear conscience and will silence any accusers.

5. Accomplishing God's will is worth any cost that evil may try and charge us.

In your journal, write down any situation in your life where you can see "good and right" overcoming a negative or harmful situation. Next, write down any circumstance you are fearful about where you need "good and right" to overcome. Lastly, write down a current setting where you know speaking truth in "gentleness and respect" could accomplish God's will.

SEPARATE OR SATURATE

Principal Kinney is on the stand, and after a well-rehearsed round of questions with Kane, it is now Tom's turn. "Ms. Kinney, what is the full name of the high school over which you preside?"

She answers, "Dr. Martin Luther King Jr. Memorial High School."

"I notice the name fails to mention Dr. King's title as 'Reverend Doctor.'"

Kinney responds, "While I realize that Dr. King had ties to the faith community—"

Tom interrupts, "Very generous of you, given that he was a Baptist minister."

She continues, "It's his work in the field of civil rights that we prefer to highlight."

"But that's the whole point—you consider his faith and politics were separate things?" Tom remarks. "But I don't. And he certainly wouldn't have."

Kane jumps to his feet. "Objection! Speculative. And counsel is testifying!"

Predictably, Stennis says, "Sustained. The jury is instructed to ignore Mr. Endler's preceding remarks."

———.———

Christian or not, we all tend to separate the sacred and the secular. In essence, this delineation means the things that have to do with God and the things that do not. In Principal Kinney's mind, she wants to ignore Martin Luther King Jr. the minister but recognize the activist and humanitarian. But the question must be asked: Can you even truly compartmentalize people in this way?

Separating God from the people and the world He created is impossible. You might deny, but you cannot remove Him. Martin Luther King Jr.'s convictions and commitments were born out of his belief. You can try to ignore his faith, but you cannot separate it from his legacy.

After Jesus had ascended to heaven and the disciples were establishing the church, there was a great divide among the people that felt much like sacred and secular. The Jews were God's chosen people and knew it, but then there were the Gentiles.

Through a vision and a miraculous moment, the apostle Peter went to the home of a centurion named Cornelius. It was unlawful for a Jew to associate with a Gentile. But, acting on a word from God, Peter went and spoke with the man's household. Scripture says the Holy Spirit came upon them all and they were baptized.

When Peter returned to Jerusalem, the other believers there criticized him, basically saying, "We cannot believe you mixed the sacred with the secular, the defiled and the holy." Listen to the end of Peter's explanation:

"As I began to speak," Peter continued, "the Holy Spirit fell on them, just as he fell on us at the beginning. Then I thought of the Lord's words when he said, 'John baptized with water, but you will be baptized with the Holy Spirit.' And since God gave these Gentiles the same gift he gave us when we believed in the Lord Jesus Christ, who was I to stand in God's way?" When the others heard this, they stopped objecting and began praising God. They said, "We can see that God has also given the Gentiles the privilege of repenting of their sins and receiving eternal life." (Acts 11:15–18 NLT)

This was the point in history when everything changed. The cultural dividing lines were falling because of the gospel. Jew and Gentile were joining hands for the first time. God was telling His leaders that when He meant salvation was for everyone, He truly meant everyone! There was no place, no one, no situation where He could be kept from moving. Someone may choose only the secular, but they can never separate from the fact that the Sacred created them.

Paul told the Romans in 3:22: "This righteousness is given through faith in Jesus Christ to all who believe. There is no difference between Jew and Gentile" (NIV).

When we make neat and tidy little divisions, this can often give us excuses for separating when we should be saturating! Our lives are saturated with Christ, so therefore our worldview is one of God being everywhere and available to everyone in every situation.

In your journal, write out how you divide the sacred from the secular in your own life by listing some examples. Then look closely at how God might be able to bring in His sacred to work in your secular. Pray and ask Him to saturate every part of your life with His Spirit.

DANGEROUS REVOLUTIONARY

Today, we continue with Principal Kinney on the stand in Grace's trial.

Tom asks, "Ms. Kinney, are you familiar with Dr. King's 'Letter from a Birmingham Jail?'"

The principal answers, "Yes, it's a seminal piece of civil rights history."

Tom presses in. "But in that letter, Dr. King makes numerous faith-based references, does he not?"

"I don't recall."

"Allow me to refresh your memory," Tom explains. "He cites the example of the three youths from the book of Daniel, who were tossed into the fiery furnace by King Nebuchadnezzar when they refused to worship him. Elsewhere he urges action with Jesus', and I quote, 'extremist love.' Is this coming back to you now?"

Kinney answers. "Yes."

Tom moves on, "And in his speech titled 'I've Been to the Mountaintop,' King stated that he just wanted to do God's will.

Ms. Kinney, in your opinion, would Ms. Wesley, had she chosen to do so, have been allowed to present those examples I just mentioned in her class?"

Kane calls out, "Objection! Speculative!"

Stennis states, "I'm going to allow it. Overruled. The witness may answer."

Kinney thinks a moment. "No. If it were up to me, she wouldn't have been allowed."

Tom asks, "Why not?"

"Because those examples are too closely associated with faith."

Tom responds, "In other words, they are facts that are *too dangerous* for discussion?"

"I wouldn't say dangerous—the word I'd use would be 'controversial.'"

Tom pops back, "But aren't facts just that? Facts? There's nothing controversial about two plus two equals four or E equals MC squared. Or the date man first landed on the moon. So why the controversy regarding these 'facts'?"

Kinney quips, "I'd say the *fact* that we're all here today speaks for itself."

Tom smiles. "Thank you for your honesty. One last question—in your orientation at the beginning of the semester, your memo to the staff stressed diversity and tolerance, did it not?"

Kinney nods. "Yes."

Tom leans in. "Would it be fair to say that, except for Christianity, all other forms of diversity are welcome?"

Kane jumps to his feet and calls out, "Objection!"

Tom snaps, "I'll withdraw the question. No further questions, Your Honor."

———·———

In three of the four gospels, we see Jesus address the men who came to arrest Him. Here is one version:

> Then Jesus spoke to the leading priests, the captains of the Temple guard, and the elders who had come for him. "Am I some dangerous revolutionary," he asked, "that you come with swords and clubs to arrest me? Why didn't you arrest me in the Temple? I was there every day. But this is your moment, the time when the power of darkness reigns." (Luke 22:52–53 NLT)

Christianity becomes dangerous in a culture when it …

1. Challenges sin.

Jesus not only shed light on sin but also redefined old ideas, such as teaching that adultery wasn't just a physical act, but is first committed in the mind. He also brought attention to not only the commission of doing wrong things, but the omission of doing right things. He became unpopular with those who did not want to change their ways and enjoyed their illicit lifestyles.

2. Questions values.

Jesus constantly taught that the value system of the kingdom of God was completely contrary to the world. He even challenged the Pharisees on upholding the law by healing people and allowing His disciples to pick grain on the Sabbath. When Jesus taught people to love God first and *all* people second, then yourself third, this was not a popular paradigm shift.

3. *Asserts truth.*

Jesus asserted His authority over the religious leaders, as well as the government, by speaking for truth, justice, and freedom. He was never afraid to speak God's truth to anyone, anywhere, at any time. This fact alone made Him quite dangerous, just as it will also make us if we truly follow Him in our own culture.

In your journal, write down somewhere you feel your faith has made you "dangerous." Next, write down somewhere you could stand to be more "dangerous." Pray and ask the Lord to show you His balance to living a "dangerous" life, following Him.

LEGACY OF LIFE AND LOVE

As Judge Stennis adjourns the court for the day, Grace manages to escape the reporters and head quietly to her car. Just as she is about to unlock the door, she looks up to see Amy, our bulldog of a blogger who's seeking the truth about God, approaching her.

Amy, as always, jumps right in. "Mind if I ask you a question? Off the record, I promise."

Grace says, "Sure."

"These people are looking to destroy you … and not just financially. Do you really think it's worth it?"

Grace pauses, searching for the best answer with her response. Finally, she says, "I hope so."

Amy, sensing the weight of the burden on Grace, responds, "So do I." Watching Grace handle this public character assassination is inspiring to Amy's own journey.

———·———

People make choices every day to die for a cause, while the world looks on and judges if it was worth it. The truth, though, is if someone has chosen to give up their freedom or life in sacrifice to something, it doesn't much matter who approves or doesn't. That's why it's called a sacrifice.

Hebrews 11 is often referred to as the "Heroes Hall of Fame" in the Bible. The names contained there are some of the finest people to ever set foot on the planet. But what made each one of them "famous" is not about them, their faith, or even what they accomplished. The common denominator for them all is the God they served.

Some very inspiring and challenging verses are found near the end of the passage.

By faith these people overthrew kingdoms, ruled with justice, and received what God had promised them. They shut the mouths of lions, quenched the flames of fire, and escaped death by the edge of the sword. Their weakness was turned to strength. They became strong in battle and put whole armies to flight. Women received their loved ones back again from death.

But others were tortured, refusing to turn from God in order to be set free. They placed their hope in a better life after the resurrection. Some were jeered at, and their backs were cut open with whips. Others were chained in prisons. Some died by stoning, some were sawed in half, and others were killed with the sword. Some went about wearing skins of sheep and goats, destitute and oppressed and mistreated. They were too good for this world, wandering over deserts and mountains, hiding in caves and holes in the ground. (Hebrews 11:33–38 NLT)

Wow! They were "too good for this world"! These words of testimony about our brothers and sisters in Christ are sobering and also indict us to ask ourselves some hard questions today. We follow an amazing legacy of commitment and sacrifice. Literally, had these people chosen not to endure all they did, we may not have ever heard the gospel.

We are very blessed to live in such an incredible day and time of modern convenience, but we also live in a day of incredible distraction from spiritual priorities. Like Grace, we must answer Amy's question: "Is it worth it?" Is Jesus worth whatever it takes to live out God's will?

Christianity—as any belief system—is only one generation away from dying. The message of the gospel is in our hands now. The "great cloud of witnesses" stands in heaven, watching what we are doing with the message for which we now have responsibility.

While you may personally never face the dilemma of having to *die* for your faith, you have the opportunity to *live* for Christ every day. You can be certain your generation knows about the One who sacrificed His life for them. *You* can be certain another generation hears the gospel.

Hebrews 11 begins with these words: "Faith is the confidence that what we hope for will actually happen; it gives us assurance about things we cannot see" (NLT). May we show the confidence in our Hope and express the assurance of that which we cannot see by deciding Jesus is indeed worth any and every sacrifice we make for Him.

Today, reread Hebrews 11 and thank God for those who endured so that you could know the gospel. Then pray for the boldness, strength, and commitment to join their legacy in your generation.

IN ENEMY TERRITORY

Pastor Dave is sitting with Reverend Jude, our constantly smiling missionary friend once again visiting stateside. We have come to love him for his always-look-on-the-God-side approach to life. The two are eating with a group of local ministers.

A senior pastor addresses the group, "Gentlemen, I don't want to spoil your brunch, but I'm hearing from a friend in the prosecutor's office about a subpoena that has just been handed down demanding all of us submit copies of our sermons from the last three months for review."

The shock of his statement silences the room. One pastor asks the obvious, "Can they do that?"

The elder pastor responds, "They tried it in Houston."

Yet another pastor chimes in. "So now the government is going to determine what we can and can't preach in our churches?"

A younger minister adds, "We might be overreacting. I'm sure there's no ill intent here."

"Really? How about no mention of Jesus allowed at US military funerals?" yet another points out.

The senior pastor warns, "Unfortunately, I think this is only the beginning, gentlemen. We've been ignoring these issues, and now we're going to pay the price for that."

One minister adds, "The silent majority is still out there. They just need something to stand for."

The younger pastor speaks again. "I'll admit there's pressure, but I think, given some time, it will correct itself."

Pastor Dave turns toward the young minister. "Forgive me, but I think you're wrong." All eyes turn to him. "I'm serving on a jury in a case right now that touches on these issues. I'm not allowed to talk about it, but frankly it scares me. And the one thing it's convinced me of? If we just sit by and do nothing, the *pressure* we're feeling today will mean *persecution* tomorrow."

The younger man challenges, "What makes you so sure?"

Pastor Dave continues, "The speed of the change and the viciousness of the opposition. The message of the gospel has us standing in the way of a lot of things that powerful people want. And our resistance to changing the message, because it's not ours to change, has made us a lot of enemies. So whether or not we admit it—we're at war. The kind of war in Ephesians 6—'not against flesh and blood but against the powers of this world and the spiritual forces of evil in the heavenly realms.' And if we insist on denying that, we've already lost."

———·———

When we hear of injustice toward Christians today, it can be so easy to make the perpetrators into the enemy. But there is no logic in blaming a non-Christian for not acting like a

Christian. What should we expect? This is exactly the reasoning and teaching that Paul was giving us in the passage Pastor Dave quoted from.

> A final word: Be strong in the Lord and in his mighty power. Put on all of God's armor so that you will be able to stand firm against all strategies of the devil. For we are not fighting against flesh-and-blood enemies, but against evil rulers and authorities of the unseen world, against mighty powers in this dark world, and against evil spirits in the heavenly places. (Ephesians 6:10–12 NLT)

We have *one* enemy in this world—Satan. People are just pawns in his plan. While we will have to disagree and deal with those who oppose our faith, we have to keep the eternal perspective of who the source of trouble truly is.

The story is told of a man who talked to his pastor about the people in his workplace who ridicule and criticize his faith. He was angry with their behavior. After hearing him vent, his pastor simply said, "Well, it sounds to me like God placed a light right in the middle of a dark room." In a moment of clarity, the man's perspective changed regarding his coworkers. They were no longer his enemies, but people God wanted him to love and serve.

Is there anyone in your life that you are viewing as "the enemy" for their behavior? Is there a situation where you are blaming people for what Satan is actually doing? Write down some ways you can change your perspective to be God's light in a dark world.

TIMELY TESTIMONY

Tom has brought Chinese takeout and all the case files to Grace's house. As they begin to eat, she asks, "So is this what you always saw yourself doing? The lawyer thing?"

"No," Tom answers in a serious tone. "I wanted to be Batman."

Grace laughs at the unexpected response.

Tom asks, "How about you? Did your parents have you all set to go to a convent?"

Grace answers, "Actually, there weren't any bedtime prayers in my childhood. I grew up in a house without faith." Her answer surprises Tom.

"So when did you decide to follow Christ?"

Grace is grateful for the opportunity to finally share her testimony with him. "One evening in college, I was walking home from class. I was really struggling at the time with a lot of things. I was scared and alone. As I turned the corner, right there in front of me was a church that had this old sign out front. I think only one of the bulbs still worked in the thing. But what it said just stopped me in my tracks. The sign read, 'Who do you say that I am?'

"And as I read it, I could hear the Lord speak to me. I couldn't get that question out of my head for days. That was the start of a journey that didn't end until I found the answer."

Tom is thoughtful, taking in Grace's deep conviction and sincerity.

———·———

Every person that has ever trusted Christ as Savior and Lord has a story. While the end result will always be the same—salvation and new life—the events leading up to the decision will always be as different and diverse as we are.

Some people grow up in Christian homes, hear the gospel many times, and then one day, make the decision to follow Christ. Others live a life of hardship, oftentimes hitting the bottom and "looking up" to find Jesus as Savior. The beauty of testimonies, however, is not at all about the circumstances, but that Christ relentlessly pursues His children through His great love and mercy.

Sometimes God speaks to our spirits through little details and unique circumstances. Everyday occurrences, such as viewing a church sign, can become miraculous invitations to eternity.

The closest we have to someone giving a testimony in Scripture is Paul's account in Philippians 3:5–9.

I am a pure-blooded citizen of Israel and a member of the tribe of Benjamin—a real Hebrew if there ever was one! I was a member of the Pharisees, who demand the strictest obedience to the Jewish law. I was so zealous that I harshly persecuted the church. And as for righteousness, I obeyed the law without fault.

I once thought these things were valuable, but now I consider them worthless because of what Christ has done. Yes, everything else is worthless when compared with the infinite value of knowing Christ Jesus my Lord. For his sake I have discarded everything else, counting it all as garbage, so that I could gain Christ and become one with him. (NLT)

Paul found out the difference between exhibiting religion for man and experiencing a relationship with Christ! Notice how he gives his credentials, then quickly tears them down to exalt Christ as the One who did the work of saving him. Paul proclaims he'll get rid of everything in his life in order to gain more of Jesus.

What if someone asked you today, *So when did you decide to follow Christ?*

How would you answer? Can you tell your story of faith? Can you concisely share the details leading up to your decision to follow Jesus?

What if that person then asked you, *So what is the answer?*

Could you tell that person how to become a Christian? *Would* you tell someone how to become a Christian?

In your journal, take a few moments to write out your testimony. You can see from both Grace's and Paul's stories, you can quickly share the circumstances of how God spoke to you and how Jesus saved you. Then, be ready to share when a "Tom" asks you, *So what is the answer?*

BLOOD LINES

M artin is alone in his dorm room one evening when his door opens and his father walks in. He has traveled across the world to confront his son about his newfound faith.

Martin, shocked, says, "Father! What are you doing here?" They begin a conversation, speaking in their native language.

His father peers out the window. "You have disgraced your family. You have chosen foolishness over reason. I have come to take you home."

Martin cannot believe what is happening and protests, "But Father!"

His dad grows angry. "You speak of this God as though He is real!"

"He is, Father! Everywhere I look, I see evidence of God's existence—His design and plan for my whole life. It's undeniable that there is a God. If you would only open your eyes, you would see."

Martin's father slaps him hard across the face and yells, "How dare you!" Now both men are feeling the deep emotion of this tragic moment. "What I see is a foolish boy who has thrown away the sacrifices that his family has made. What you have done is unforgivable."

Martin begins to regain strength, saying, "I've done what I had to do." He turns and looks his father in the eyes. "God has spoken to me, father, and I have listened."

His dad, now realizing what his own culture demands him to do as a parent, asks, "So you would disobey? You will throw away everything for Him?"

"Father, I would," Martin says quietly.

His dad, growing more emotional, begins to walk toward the door. Finally, he says, "Then … you are no longer … my son." He walks out—forever.

Martin calls out after him, "Father!"

———·———

One of the most difficult passages from Jesus' teaching is found in Matthew 10:32–39. This is one of those uncomfortable sections we often prefer not to think about, much less read.

> "Whoever acknowledges me before others, I will also acknowledge before my Father in heaven. But whoever disowns me before others, I will disown before my Father in heaven. Do not suppose that I have come to bring peace to the earth. I did not come to bring peace, but a sword. For I have come to turn 'a man against his father, a daughter against her mother, a daughter-in-law against her mother-in-law—a man's enemies will be the members of his own household.' Anyone who loves their father or mother more than me is not worthy of me; anyone who loves their son

or daughter more than me is not worthy of me. Whoever does not take up their cross and follow me is not worthy of me. Whoever finds their life will lose it, and whoever loses their life for my sake will find it" (NIV).

Whether today or in Jesus' time, people seem to either love Him deeply or hate Him with a passion. Consider His own circle—Peter was willing to die for Him, while Judas was selling Him out to be crucified.

Why did, and why does, Jesus create such controversy and division? Because He came to make the ultimate distinction between light and darkness; He did not come to bring peace, but a sword!

If Christ Himself caused such reactions, you will see similar responses at times to your faith in Him. People will question, reject, and criticize you for your faith. But on the contrary, some people will be drawn to Christ in you.

Jesus knew that even though He brings peace to individuals, His presence also produces conflict. Light will always clash with darkness. People who choose not to believe in God will always be at odds with those who have become His children—even when they are in the same family.

In verses 37–38, Jesus is using an overstatement, an exaggeration, a common device that rabbis used to make a point. He is not at all saying we are to hate our family, but yet that we should love Him so much that any other love seems like hate by comparison.

Think about your most important relationships. Who accepts your faith, who simply tolerates it, and who rejects you for your belief? In your journal, write down those names and, today, whether friend or foe, pray for each one.

CRUCIAL CROSSROADS

Late at night inside St. James Church, Martin sinks into one of the pews in the darkness. Still reeling and heartbroken over his father's visiting him by surprise and asking him to deny his faith, his single burning question was what God could possibly want from him. In that moment, Martin realizes a single beam of light is shining down on the baby grand piano on the stage.

Now seated, playing and singing the simple melody of "Nearer My God to Thee," the worship he feels in his spirit begins to move him to tears. Supernatural strength and hope are being infused into this new believer. Ending the song and sensing God speak to him, in his native tongue he says the words meaning, "So that's it."

Suddenly, from the back of the church, Brooke appears. "That was beautiful." She had slipped in and been listening for a while.

With his eyes still full of tears, Martin says, "Forgive me. I did not know anyone was here."

Brooke responds, "Please don't apologize." She is holding

her brother's Bible. "I didn't mean to interrupt. I just didn't know anywhere else to go."

Martin looks at the cross on the platform. "I understand."

"I just felt like I needed to come here. And then when I heard you playing, I knew I was right where I was supposed to be."

He smiles and offers his hand. "I'm Martin."

"I'm Brooke. Do you think I could ask you a few questions?"

As the tables are now ironically turned, Martin can't help but smile. "That would be fine."

Brooke, relieved, adds, "Good, because I have a lot of them."

———·———

In Acts 8, we find a similar story. An angel told Philip to walk down a certain road. He came upon the treasurer of Ethiopia, headed back home after being in Jerusalem to worship.

Seated in his carriage, he was reading aloud from the book of the prophet Isaiah. The Holy Spirit said to Philip, "Go over and walk along beside the carriage." Philip ran over and heard the man reading from the prophet Isaiah. Philip asked, "Do you understand what you are reading?" The man replied, "How can I, unless someone instructs me?" And he urged Philip to come up into the carriage and sit with him. … So beginning with this same Scripture, Philip told him the Good News about Jesus. As they rode along, they came to some water, and the eunuch said, "Look! There's some water! Why can't I be baptized?" He ordered the carriage to stop, and they went down into the water, and Philip baptized him. (vv. 28–31, 35–38 NLT)

We can glean two important points from Brooke and Martin's story as well as Philip and the Ethiopian's account in Scripture.

1. The Holy Spirit navigates the salvation journey.
Martin was drawn to the church, and to the piano, at the same time that Brooke felt compelled to go to the church. Philip was led to the Ethiopian to answer his questions and bring him to Christ.

While we certainly must always be prepared to share our faith, we must also remember the Holy Spirit is the One actually doing the work. We are simply the messengers.

2. From the moment of salvation, God can work through you.
If you asked Martin if he was ready to take Pastor Dave's role and be the one answering questions, he would have said, *Absolutely not.* But God thought otherwise. The next step of growth for Martin was to share what he had experienced with Brooke.

Having the privilege of being involved in the salvation process for others is one of the greatest joys we can ever experience in life.

Whether you are as mature and ready as Philip or as new and uncertain as Martin, write down the names of a few people in your circles that you know need to hear the gospel. Close today by praying for God to give you "ears to hear" when He speaks.

DEITY DOT CONNECTING

With the takeout containers now empty, Grace and Tom are combing through the case files. Tom suddenly grits out, "He doesn't make mistakes!" referring to Attorney Kane.

Grace responds, "But I thought you proved bias?"

Tom comes back, "Principal Kinney and Ms. Rizzo? Those were jabs. We need a knockout punch. Why did you feel so compelled to bring up Jesus in a history class anyway, Grace?"

"Well, why *shouldn't* I have?"

Tom regains his composure. "Grace, I'm not here to debate the—"

"No. Listen. This really isn't about faith. This is about history. Maybe I'm wrong. I mean, I'm not the law expert here, but it seems like they've missed the point. Their whole attack is about me 'preaching in class.' But I didn't."

Tom interjects, "They'll say you did. You cited Scripture and talked about Jesus' teachings as if they were just like any other verifiable fact."

"But what if they are just that?" Grace asks, as she begins to connect the dots. "Just because certain facts happen to be recorded in the Bible doesn't mean they stop being facts. We can separate the fact-based elements of Jesus' life from the faith-based elements. In my classroom, I didn't talk about Jesus as my Lord and Savior. All I did was comment on quotations attributed to Jesus, the man." Tom is beginning to see Grace's logic as she adds, "And I did it during AP History. There was nothing wrong with the context."

He jumps in. "Any rule saying you can talk about every human being who ever existed except for Jesus is discriminatory. The school board can't institute it."

Grace completes his thought. "And every credible historian admits that Jesus existed. There's just too much evidence!"

They both pause, realizing they are onto something. Tom's mood totally changes. "Grace, I love it. That's our defense— Jesus as a historical figure like everybody else. And you know what? Kane will never see it coming."

Grace walks over to her bookshelf, scanning the spines until she finds *Man, Myth, or Messiah* by Dr. Rice Broocks. She takes the book down and hands it to Tom. "You've got some reading to do."

—— · ——

One day Jesus said to his disciples, "Let's cross to the other side of the lake." So they got into a boat and started out. As they sailed across, Jesus settled down for a nap. But soon a fierce storm came down on the lake. The boat was filling with water, and they were in real danger. The disciples went and woke him up, shouting, "Master, Master, we're going to drown!" When Jesus woke up, he rebuked the wind and the raging waves. Suddenly the storm stopped and all was calm. Then he asked them, "Where is your faith?" The disciples were terrified and amazed. "Who is this man?" they asked each other. "When he gives a command, even the wind and waves obey him!" (Luke 8:22–25 NLT)

To the disciples, Jesus was not only quite real, but they also knew He was a rabbi with an incredible ability to teach. In fact, this could have been a strong motivation for these Jewish men who understood the value of a rabbi asking them to follow Him as their teacher and mentor. But as they began to see evidence of something much greater going on, the questions started coming.

This event was life changing for these men. They went from being afraid of the storm to being terrified of watching a man stop a storm!

There is a very similar moment in our lives when we, too, see, hear, and understand Jesus is who He said He is. No, you likely didn't watch any wind and waves stopped in their tracks, but maybe He calmed a personal storm for you. Something happened that you could not explain or deny and you were convinced about Jesus. He went from just a man in history, or even a myth, to *your* Messiah.

In your journal, write down any "storm-stopper" moments you have had where you know Jesus was at work. Close by thanking Him for those and also the ones that are coming in your life, because they certainly will. Why? Because He is who He said He is.

CLAIMING CLARITY

Martin and Brooke are sitting in a pew at the church, talking late at night. Brooke shares, "Carter had written so many notes in the margin of his Bible that for the first time I felt like I was truly getting to know my brother. Like, God gave me the extra five minutes that I so desperately needed with him. I just don't understand why he never told me about his faith."

Martin smiles knowingly. "Sharing one's faith with family, especially not knowing how they will react, can be difficult."

Brooke responds, "Count our struggles as a blessing, right?"

"That is exactly right." Inspired now to overflowing, Martin turns to Brooke. "There are more than five minutes awaiting you and your brother. John 11:25–26 states, 'I am the Resurrection and the Life. He who believes in me will live, even if he dies. And whoever lives and believes in me will never die. Do you believe this?'"

Brooke, clearly moved by his words and invitation, answers, "I do."

Martin continues, "Then invite Him into your heart and

make Him the Lord of your life." The two, connected in this holy moment, bow their heads.

Brooke begins to pray—for the first time in her life. "Dear Lord, I'm not quite sure what to say, but ... thank You for dying on the cross for me. Please forgive me of my sin. Jesus, please come into my life, and I will follow You as my Lord and Savior."

Martin says, "Amen."

Brooke wipes away tears of joy. "Thank you."

In that moment, life begins to make sense to Martin like it never has before. There is a clarity he grabs hold of deep down in his soul. His calling has come. He knows his purpose and what God wants of him—to return to his own country to become a pastor and lead many to faith, just as he did with Brooke. Martin knows Jesus does the saving, but he wants to join Him as His messenger in that work to his own people, who so desperately need to know the truth.

———·———

Even the disciples had to come to their own moments of belief as to who Jesus was, and then to their own calling to His ministry.

One of the twelve disciples, Thomas (nicknamed the Twin), was not with the others when Jesus came. They told him, "We have seen the Lord!" But he replied, "I won't believe it unless I see the nail wounds in his hands, put my fingers into them, and place my hand into the wound in his side." Eight days later the disciples were together again, and this time Thomas was with them. The doors were locked; but suddenly, as before, Jesus was standing among them. "Peace be with you," he said. Then he said to Thomas, "Put your finger here, and look at my hands. Put your hand into the wound in my side. Don't be faithless any longer. Believe!" "My Lord and my God!" Thomas exclaimed. Then Jesus told him, "You believe because you have seen me. Blessed are those who believe without seeing me." (John 20:24–29 NIV)

We have the great advantage of knowing the entire story of Jesus from start to finish. The disciples were living this out moment by moment, miracle by miracle. Because of this difference in perspective, we often judge our spiritual forefathers too harshly. Even calling Thomas "doubting" isn't fair. Take a look at what he says when he realizes Jesus is standing before him: "My Lord and my God!" What an incredible moment of clarity and worship.

Today's passage reminds us that whether we are locked away and hiding as Brooke had been or have the doors wide open like Martin, Jesus can get to us as His children. Even when we close doors to everyone in our life, Jesus is on the inside with us. And when He comes, He will always say, "Peace be with you. Don't be faithless any longer. Believe!"

Do you relate more to Brooke today—searching for faith—or to Martin—seeking God's calling? In your journal, write down any area where you feel you need Jesus to provide evidence that He is alive and working in your life. Remember: He is always, always with you!

DAY 31

ETERNAL EVIDENCE

S tarting a fresh day in court with a renewed confidence and approach, Tom asks his witness, "Can you state your name and occupation for the court?"

"My name is Lee Strobel. I'm a professor of Christian thought at Houston Baptist University and the author of *The Case for Christ*."

Tom continues, "Can you help me prove the existence of Jesus Christ?"

Strobel responds, "Absolutely. Beyond any reasonable doubt."

"How so?"

"Historian Gary Habermas lists thirty-nine ancient sources for Jesus, from which he enumerates more than one hundred recorded facts about his life, teaching, crucifixion, and resurrection. In fact, the historical evidence of Jesus' execution is so strong that one of the most famous New Testament scholars in the world, Gerd Ludemann, said, 'Jesus' death as a consequence of crucifixion is indisputable.' Now, there are very few facts in ancient history that a critical historian like

Ludemann will say are 'indisputable.' One of them is the execution of Jesus Christ."

Tom then asks, "Forgive me, but as a Bible-believing Christian, wouldn't this tend to inflate your estimate of the probability that Jesus existed?"

Strobel answers, "No, because we don't need to inflate it. We can reconstruct the basic facts about Jesus just from non-Christian sources outside the Bible. Gerd Ludemann is an atheist. In other words, we can prove the existence of Jesus solely by using sources that have absolutely no sympathy toward Christianity. As the agnostic historian, Bart Ehrman, says, 'Jesus did exist whether we like it or not.' I put it this way: denying the existence of Jesus doesn't make Him go away; it merely proves no amount of evidence will convince you."

Tom concludes, "No further questions, Your Honor."

"Mr. Kane, your witness."

Kane quietly responds, "No questions, Your Honor."

—·—

As Christians, we can forget that Jesus' life and death is also a matter of historical record. This is exactly why non-Christians can believe Jesus was a prophet or a great teacher. They view His life as real, but outside of the realm of faith.

We must also remember that there are those outside of faith who know the Bible very well. We may have come to view God's Word as a love letter, while some only see it as a textbook. The difference is we have found a relationship within the pages.

After Jesus' death on the cross, we read some intriguing responses from eyewitnesses:

1. Centurion at the cross

Just after Jesus gave up His life to the Father (Matthew 27:50), the next few verses (51–53) contain some epic episodes—an earthquake, tombs splitting open, and dead people rising. One of the centurions overseeing Christ's execution is documented in verse 54 as saying, "Surely he was the Son of God!" Was this man one of His torturers, one of the mockers, only minutes before? We don't know those details, but we do know his mind was changed quickly by what he witnessed firsthand.

2. Joseph of Arimethea

He was obviously a man of means and reputation to own his own tomb and to be able to request access to Jesus' body directly from Pilate. He, along with the two Marys, prepared Christ's body for burial and placed Him in the tomb (Matthew 27:57–61). We do know that Joseph was a disciple inside Jesus' circle, involved with His entombment. Is it possible that Joseph believed in Jesus to the point of knowing he was only *loaning* his tomb for three days?

3. Guards at the tomb

It is quite ironic that the Pharisees asked Pilate to place guards at Jesus' tomb in case the disciples were planning a hoax, but they were unknowingly planting eyewitnesses. They didn't want to take any chances on further harming their reputations, but on the morning of the third day, those guards had the privilege of witnessing the greatest moment in human history—the resurrection. Matthew 28:4 states, "The guards were so afraid of him that they shook and became like dead men."

While our relationship with Jesus as Savior is based on

faith, the gospel is also a matter of history and records that back up what we know to be true about Jesus, as we see in the testimonies in Grace's trial. Our house of belief is indeed built on a solid foundation of facts!

An important way to keep your faith fresh is to regularly read the gospels. The more we know of Scripture, the better we can share with those who have questions. Consider starting a daily reading plan through the gospels the day after you finish this devotional book.

PRESSURE POINTS

Pastor Dave's thoughts go back to the pastors' gathering and the discussion regarding the subpoena for local ministers to submit their recent sermons for governmental review. He's stepping up to the county clerk's desk as a response to his own letter he received at the church.

"My name is Reverend David Hill," he states.

The clerk responds, "Sermon transcripts, right? Put them right there, please. They've been coming in all morning."

Dave scans an impressive stack of envelopes and folders. "I'm sure they did what they felt was right." He hands a letter to the clerk, written in the wee hours of the morning at his office, on the same night Martin was playing "Nearer My God to Thee" in the sanctuary.

The man looks surprised. "That's it? This is all your sermons from the last three months?"

Reverend Dave responds, "No, this is the letter I wrote, explaining why I'm not going to hand them over."

The clerk, surprise now turning to shock, says, "Excuse me?"

Dave answers, "I know it's unusual for a Christian pastor to willfully resist a subpoena issued by a lawful governmental authority. It's even more unusual that he should feel compelled to do so."

"Are you sure you want to do that?" the clerk asks.

"I feel it's something that I have to do," Dave affirms.

The man nods and says, "You know the old saying, 'The squeaky wheel gets the grease'? Well, I have a different saying: 'A nail that sticks up … gets hammered down.'"

———·———

The apostle Paul became quite familiar with his stand for Christ upsetting the government. The platforms in court became Paul's pulpits!

About eight or ten days later Festus returned to Caesarea, and on the following day he took his seat in court and ordered that Paul be brought in. When Paul arrived, the Jewish leaders from Jerusalem gathered around and made many serious accusations they couldn't prove. Paul denied the charges. "I am not guilty of any crime against the Jewish laws or the Temple or the Roman government," he said. Then Festus, wanting to please the Jews, asked him, "Are you willing to go to Jerusalem and stand trial before me there?" But Paul replied, "No! This is the official Roman court, so I ought to be tried right here. You know very well I am not guilty of harming the Jews. If I have done something worthy of death, I don't refuse to die. But if I am innocent, no one has a right to turn me over to these men to kill me. I appeal to Caesar!"

Festus conferred with his advisers and then replied, "Very well! You have appealed to Caesar, and to Caesar you will go!" (Acts 25:6–12 NLT)

A simple definition of "civil disobedience" is the active and verbal refusal to obey a law or command. Thomas Jefferson said, "If a law is unjust, a man is not only right to disobey it, he is obligated to do so." Martin Luther King Jr. is quoted as saying, "One has a moral responsibility to disobey unjust laws." The connotation of this phrase always has to do with a person believing and adhering to a higher law than the government. For a person to enact civil disobedience, their worldview is conflicting with human authority.

Every day we see the cultural boundary lines being pulled in tighter and tighter on faith. As the government legislates ideas that run contrary to God's law in Scripture, the day is rapidly approaching when some issue will arrive at each of our doorsteps and demand standing up or bowing down.

When pressure becomes persecution, we will find out how committed we are to our faith in Christ. Has it just been a social exercise inherited from childhood that can be easily tossed aside, or a submitted engagement with the Living God that could never be denied? As the days grow darker—make no mistake—the lines will be drawn. We are living in the season of deciding where we stand and building up for the battle.

In your journal, write down what you believe to be your strong points as a Christian. Next, list a few areas you know you need to strengthen and grow. What steps can you take today to be ready for anything God calls you to tomorrow?

DELIGHT, DESIRES, AND DOORWAYS

While Pastor Dave is involved in Grace's court case, Reverend Jude is holding down the fort at the church. He looks up to see Amy walking into the sanctuary. "Can I help you with something?"

Feeling a bit awkward, Amy responds, "I'm looking for Pastor Dave. My ex-boyfriend's sister, Mina, told me he was wonderful and I should come see him. She said he's really easy to talk to."

Reverend Jude explains, "Well, he's not here. He won't be back until after next week."

Amy, obviously disappointed, says, "Oh, Okay. Thanks." She turns to leave.

"If you need to talk, I'm actually a pastor," Jude says. The two take a seat on a pew in the sanctuary and quickly begin to share freely.

"It's been three weeks since my doctor told me I'm in remission, but even though I've been given this gift, I've been questioning my faith. I know Jesus existed, but I'm struggling to believe," Amy confesses.

Reverend Jude smiles and reassures, "Actually, I think you already do believe. And the proof is that you're not willing to put God back on the shelf now that your cancer is gone. He won't let you dismiss the thought of Him. Part of you senses Jesus' presence and wishes He would just go away and leave you alone."

Amy agrees. "I have to admit, I've had that thought."

"But He loves you too much to do that," the reverend states. Amy is obviously deep in thought and evaluating his words when he says, "He delights in using us in ways we never dreamed and giving us things we never even knew we wanted. We just have to give Him the chance. Will you?"

———·———

Everyone who asks will receive. Everyone who searches will find. And the door will be opened for everyone who knocks. Would any of you give your hungry child a stone, if the child asked for some bread? Would you give your child a snake if the child asked for a fish? As bad as you are, you still know how to give good gifts to your children. But your heavenly Father is even more ready to give good things to people who ask. (Matthew 7:8–11 CEV)

The battle in the garden of Eden forever planted a seed of doubt in mankind. Because of the enemy's work on Adam and Eve, questioning God on every level of relationship became normal on that day. But even when God forever made things right with His creation through Christ's work on the cross, He still offered us the free will and choice to make a decision for ourselves.

We have watched Amy struggle with life and death, desperation and doubt, but we have also seen her tenacious desire to reconcile her faith to personal peace.

Verse 8 is a constant encouragement to proactively ask, search, and knock to know God in deeper ways. But the promise just gets better in verse 11—the heavenly Father is "ready to give good things."

Let's be quite clear, it does *not* say what so many seem to believe about God: He is ready to withhold and take things away because we blew it. That is still a part of the lie implanted in our DNA in the garden. Those images and ideas of God are exactly what the enemy wants us to believe so we *won't* ask, search, and knock. Why? Because the Enemy knows God has good gifts for His children, and he doesn't want us to receive them!

What about you? Do you relate to the concept of believing God would give you a rock when you ask for bread? Or even something as twisted as giving you a snake when you ordered fish? If either of these lies has infected you, decide today to believe the truth Christ taught us in Matthew 7.

Your Heavenly Father wants you to…

receive from Him.

find all He has for you.

walk through every door that He opens for you.

open every good gift He gives you.

In your journal, write down a few of the things (material or spiritual) you have received from Him lately. Inventory your life and look for any door or gift He may have in front of you that you need to open.

I-WITNESS

B ack at Grace's trial, Tom calls his next witness to the stand. He begins, "Would you state your name and experience for the record?"

"James Warner Wallace—former homicide detective for the County of Los Angeles. I was on the force for more than twenty-five years."

Tom: "And are you the author of the book *Cold-Case Christianity*?"

Wallace: "I am."

Tom: "Could you also state the book's subtitle for the court?"

Wallace: "A Homicide Detective Investigates the Claims of the Gospels."

Tom: "Would I be correct in saying that your duties consisted of investigating 'cold-case' homicides?"

Wallace: "You would. That was my area of expertise."

Tom: "What is the most common way those cases get solved?"

Wallace: "Often, by carefully examining witness testimony years earlier at the time of the crime. Even though by the time of our reinvestigation the witnesses, and often the officers who first took their statements, are now deceased."

Tom: "Forgive me, Mr. Wallace, but how is that even possible?"

Wallace: "There are a number of techniques available to us when testing the reliability of eyewitness statements. One approach is to employ Forensic Statement Analysis. That's the discipline of scrutinizing a witness' statements and what they choose to stress, minimize, or omit completely. Their choices of pronouns, verb tenses, descriptions of what they saw and heard, how they compress or expand time—it's all revealing. By going back and closely inspecting the testimony of various witnesses, noting the correlations, separating seeming inconsistencies from actual inconsistencies, then we can often figure out who's telling the truth, who's lying, and who the guilty party is."

Tom: "And did you apply this skill set anytime outside of your official capacity?"

Wallace: "Yes, I decided to approach the death of Jesus at the hands of the Romans using my experience as a cold-case detective. I approached the Gospels as I would any other forensic statement. Every word was important to me. Every little idiosyncrasy stood out."

Tom: "And what did you conclude?"

Wallace: "Within a matter of months, as I tested the Gospels from a cold-case perspective, I concluded that all four accounts were written from different perspectives, containing unique details that are specific to eyewitnesses."

———·———

The concept of eyewitnesses and their accounts is actually quite prevalent throughout the New Testament. In Luke 24,

Jesus referred to the prophecies about Him and ended by saying, "You are witnesses of all these things" (v. 48 NLT). He was connecting the fact that what the Old Testament scrolls said about him, that they had all read, they were now seeing firsthand. What an amazing time to be alive and an incredible place to be! But the most notable aspect of this verse is *when* it takes place. These are the words of the resurrected Christ! He has defeated death and the grave, while now giving them eyewitness testimony.

Earlier in Jesus' ministry, some of the Jewish leaders had confronted Him about His actions. He responded to their accusations.

> If I were to testify on my own behalf, my testimony would not be valid. But someone else is also testifying about me, and I assure you that everything he says about me is true. In fact, you sent investigators to listen to John the Baptist, and his testimony about me was true. Of course, I have no need of human witnesses, but I say these things so you might be saved. (John 5:31–34 NLT)

In effect here, Jesus was saying He did not need witnesses to prove His existence and authority, because God had firmly established that already. The purpose of eyewitnesses wasn't to provide proof *to* man, but to spread the gospel of salvation *for* man.

Grace's trial is not really about having to prove God's existence, but rather displaying God's power! This is also the very goal of our lives.

In your journal, write down a couple of eyewitness accounts where you have seen God at work firsthand. Remember: while you are His witness to speak your testimony, you are also a constant eyewitness to His power.

INTERCONNECTED COMMUNITY

Today, we pick back up with Tom's questioning of James Warner Wallace, former homicide detective and author of the book *Cold-Case Christianity*.

Tom: "Did you consider the idea that the four gospel accounts might be part of a conspiracy designed to promote belief in a fledgling faith?"

Wallace: "Of course. It's one of the first things you consider with any set of witness statements, and I've investigated many conspiracy cases. There are several common characteristics of successful conspiracies, however, and I don't find any of these attributes were present in the first century for those who claimed to be witnesses of Jesus' life, ministry, and resurrection."

Tom: "Can you explain some of these attributes for us?"

Wallace: "The problem with conspiracy theories related to the first Christians is there were simply too many of them, having to tell and keep the lie for too long, separated by thousands of miles without any modern ability to communicate with each other quickly. Worse yet, they were pressured beyond words.

They suffered and died for their testimony. Not a single one ever recanted their claims, even in this impossibly difficult environment. Conspiracy theories related to the apostles are simply unreasonable, and they aren't reflected in the nature of the gospels. What I see, instead, are attributes of reliable eyewitness accounts, including numerous examples of what I refer to as 'unintended eyewitness support statements.'"

Tom: "And what is that?"

Wallace: "There are times when one witness' statement raises more questions than it answers. But when we eventually talk to the next witness, the second one will unintentionally provide us with some detail making sense of the first witness' statement. True eyewitness statements often include this kind of support."

Tom: "Can you give us an example of this in the Gospels?"

Wallace: "In describing Jesus' examination before the former high priest, Caiaphas, on the night before his crucifixion, Matthew's gospel states: 'Then they spat in His face and beat Him with their fists; and others slapped Him, and said, "Prophesy to us, you Christ; who is the one who hit You?"' [26:67–68 NASB]. This question seems odd since Jesus' attackers were standing right in front of him. Why would they ask Him, 'Who is the one who hit you?' It doesn't seem like much of a challenge until we read what Luke tells us: 'Now the men who were holding Jesus in custody were mocking Him and beating Him; and they blindfolded Him and were asking Him, saying, "Prophesy, who is the one who hit You?"' [22:63–64 NASB]. So one gospel eyewitness unintentionally supports the other. That's an example of interconnectedness."

Tom: "And how would you best summarize the overall results of your research?"

Wallace: "After years of intense scrutiny and applying a template I use to determine if eyewitnesses are reliable, I conclude that the four gospels in this book contain the reliable accounts of the actual words of Jesus."

Tom: "To include the statements quoted by Ms. Wesley in her classroom?"

Wallace: "Yes. Absolutely."

———·———

Seeing the Gospels through Wallace's professional experience is fascinating. This also brings up an important point regarding the Bible.

We all read Scripture through the lens of our own background and experience as well as emotional, mental, and spiritual needs at the time. This is one of the best aspects of taking part in a small group or Bible class. Discussing Scripture inside a community of believers can challenge and inspire us to see and hear important points we might never understand otherwise. Hearing from different points of view can sharpen and deepen us like no other form of discipleship.

Who challenges you the most in Scripture reading and study? Why does this person impact your view? Is it their knowledge or perspective or maybe both? Is there someone in your life that you challenge in this way? Why do you have this impact on that person?

On a previous day, we looked at your filters for relationships. Today, write down the filters through which you read Scripture. Think through your own background and experiences to discover your unique "attributes" — how you take in God's Word. There may be some filters you need to fully support, while others might need to be dropped as you grow.

RIGHTEOUS INTERRUPTION

Kane begins his questioning of James Warner Wallace. "Detective, I'm not going to try to match Bible knowledge with you, but isn't it true the gospel accounts vary widely in what they say? Aren't there numerous discrepancies between the accounts?"

Wallace: "Absolutely. Which is exactly what we'd expect."

Kane: "I'm not sure I understand."

Wallace: "Reliable eyewitnesses always differ slightly in their accounts. When two or more witnesses see the same event, they usually experience it differently and focus on different aspects of the action. Their statements are greatly influenced by their unique interests, backgrounds, and perspectives. My goal in assessing the Gospels was simply to determine whether they represented valid, reliable, eyewitness testimony, in spite of any apparent differences between accounts."

Kane: "And as a devout Christian, you feel you succeeded?"

Wallace: "Mr. Kane, I'm afraid you misunderstand me.

When I started my study, I was a devout atheist. I approached the Gospels as a dedicated skeptic, not as a believer."

Kane did not see this coming. As he is speechless, Wallace continues, "I wasn't raised in a Christian environment, but I think I have an unusually high amount of respect for evidence. I'm not a Christian today because I was raised that way, because it satisfies some need, or accomplishes some goal. I'm simply a Christian because it's evidentially true."

Kane finds his words. "Motion to strike, Your Honor!"

Judge Stennis is just as shocked. "Granted. The jury is instructed to ignore Detective Wallace's last remarks."

Kane closes. "No further questions."

But the jury can't possibly unhear the amazing testimony they have just heard.

———·———

For every person who has come to salvation in Christ, God has brought evidence of Himself that provided the faith to believe. He orchestrates events and circumstances just as He did for James Warner Wallace.

Perhaps the most disturbing but divine salvation encounter in Scripture was someone much farther away from God than Wallace was as an atheist investigator.

Jesus and his disciples had pulled up to shore in their boat. A man filled with many demons named Legion, who had been living in a nearby cemetery and cutting himself with stones, came running up to them. Imagine that frightening scene! Somehow he knew the only One who could deliver and save him. Jesus cast every last demon out into a herd of pigs, which then ran into the lake and drowned.

The herdsmen fled to the nearby town and the surrounding countryside, spreading the news as they ran. People rushed out to see what had happened. A crowd soon gathered around Jesus, and they saw the man who had been possessed by the legion of demons. He was sitting there fully clothed and perfectly sane. ...

As Jesus was getting into the boat, the man who had been demon possessed begged to go with him. But Jesus said, "No, go home to your family, and tell them everything the Lord has done for you and how merciful he has been." So the man started off to visit the Ten Towns of that region and began to proclaim the great things Jesus had done for him; and everyone was amazed at what he told them. (Mark 5:14–15, 18–20 NLT)

The most fascinating thing about this story is the evidence that Jesus can deliver, heal, save, and redeem anyone! An army of demons, a soul full of anger, a damaged past, or years of deceived ideas about the existence of God cannot stop the Lord.

Just as Wallace and the delivered man were not too far gone to be reached by Jesus' love and healing, you also were not. Take a moment to list out a few of the roadblocks and sins God had to overcome to get to you. Think through how God could use those as you share with others who could relate to *your* testimony.

MESSAGE AND MISSION

B rooke is called to the witness stand and, after Tom's questioning, all appears to be going well. Then Kane begins, and after some comfortable back-and-forth, the plot twists.

Kane: "Do you think there's any possibility that in answering your question in class, Ms. Wesley might have been looking to share her ideas about faith?"

Brooke: "No ... not at that moment."

Kane: "Not at that moment? Do you mean there were other times in which Ms. Wesley did speak to you about her faith?"

"Yes ... but it was outside of school ... and it was only one time."

Tom jumps to his feet. "Move to strike! Your Honor, this is irrelevant. No actions off the school campus are at issue here."

Stennis responds, "Denied. Mr. Kane seems to have found a loose thread, and I'm inclined to let him pull it to see what unravels."

Kane continues, "Brooke, can you explain what you meant about discussing faith outside of school?"

"My brother died in an accident six months ago. Ms. Wesley noticed I wasn't doing so well and, after class, asked me if everything was all right. I told her I was fine, but then I went and found her at the coffee shop later."

Kane: "So what did Ms. Wesley do?"

Brooke answers, "She was nice. We talked for a long time. I could tell she really cared. I asked her how she kept it together so well, and she said it was Jesus."

Kane: "So she's the one who brought up Jesus. And did her endorsement lead you into exploring Christianity?"

Brooke: "Yes, at first. But when the Salvation Army came to pick up my brother's things, one of the workers found his Bible and gave it to me. I didn't even know he had one. So I started reading. And once I started, I realized I didn't want to stop. That's why I came up with the question I asked in class."

Kane: "So then, without Ms. Wesley's direct influence, you never would have asked the question that put us all here in the first place, would you? And based on your readings, would you now consider yourself a 'believer'?"

Brooke answers yes.

Kane presses harder. "Maybe even a 'Christian'?"

Brooke once again answers yes.

Kane moves in for the kill. "Brooke, is it likely that any of this—your Bible reading, your question about Jesus in class, or your newfound commitment to Christianity—would have come about without Ms. Wesley's direct involvement?"

Brooke responds, "No. It wouldn't."

———·———

All these new things are from God who brought us back to himself through what Christ Jesus did. And

God has given us the privilege of urging everyone to come into his favor and be reconciled to him. For God was in Christ, restoring the world to himself, no longer counting men's sins against them but blotting them out. This is the wonderful message he has given us to tell others. We are Christ's ambassadors. (2 Corinthians 5:18–20 TLB)

What Grace is "guilty" of is what every Christ follower should also be about—being available to meet people's needs and share about Jesus.

In all your circles of influence, God's plan for them to hear about His offer of salvation is through just one messenger—you! He doesn't need a slick program, a cool video presentation, or an articulate preacher as long as He has you and your story of redemption. God longs for you to be the one to take His message to those around you.

Like governments appoint ambassadors to live on foreign soil to represent their interests in other nations, God has appointed you to represent Him to the mission field around you. While you may doubt your ability to be an effective witness for Him, you need to understand that He isn't questioning you. In fact, after He saved you, He left you here just so you can lead others to Him by your life, example, and words. How's that for a life calling and motivation?

Take a few minutes to list the "mission fields" where God has uniquely and strategically placed you. Are you offering up any excuses as to your effectiveness for Christ? Reread today's passage and ask God to give you an ever-increasing strength and boldness for Him.

WHEN GOD WHISPERS

Back at home, Grace carries a large cupcake to the table with one lone candle. She sits it down in front of Walter. "Happy birthday, Grandpa. Sorry it's not much of a celebration."

Walter smiles and quips, "Any time you let me near icing, it's a celebration." He blows out the candle, and both of them grab a spoon to dig into the impromptu birthday cake.

Grace confesses, "I was praying in my room earlier and it's funny, but it's like Jesus isn't letting me feel His presence. Usually it's like I can almost reach out and touch Him … but right now? It's like He's a million miles away, and I can't make out a word of what He's saying … or if He's even saying anything at all."

Walter responds, "Grace, you of all people should realize that when you're going through something really hard, remember: the teacher is always quiet during the test." The words strike Grace with wisdom and give her comfort.

Just then, there's a knock at the front door. Grace and Walter go out to see who is there. A group of students are standing outside, each one holding a single lit candle.

Grace sees Brooke among the familiar faces. She is still

reeling from her well-meaning testimony after being grilled on the witness stand by Kane. The entire group begins to sing the worshipful hymn "How Great Thou Art." Walter joins in with the singing, and Grace is brought to tears by this heartfelt and Spirit-led display of worship and friendship.

———·———

The prophet Elijah had just seen God rain fire from heaven right on cue and completely consume the altar, shutting down the 450 prophets of Baal. Then Elijah oversaw their execution. It appears to be a spiritual and strategic victory, fully from the hand of God, right? But how quickly we can become discouraged when circumstances change.

Jezebel found out what Elijah had done and sent him a message that said, *Within the next twenty-four hours, I will do to you what you did to them!* Regardless of what he had seen God do, he ran, becoming depressed and apathetic. Eventually, he laid down and said, "God, take me now. I've had enough." But the Almighty ignored the whining and instead fed him.

Elijah then journeyed on, wandering around for forty days, ending up in the cleft of a rock. God asked, "Elijah, what are you doing here?" Just like with Adam, as a loving Father, He asked, "Why are you hiding?" Elijah vindicated himself and blamed Israel for the issues.

The LORD said, "Go out and stand on the mountain in the presence of the LORD, for the LORD is about to pass by." Then a great and powerful wind tore the mountains apart and shattered the rocks before the

LORD, but the LORD was not in the wind. After the wind there was an earthquake, but the LORD was not in the earthquake. After the earthquake came a fire, but the LORD was not in the fire. And after the fire came a gentle whisper. (1 Kings 19:11–12 NIV)

God then tells Elijah to get back on the road, go back to work, and that He will provide help.

When Grace's situation was looking like the worst could happen, she sensed a distance from God. Walter's point to her was a nugget of wisdom for us all. So often, as in Elijah's circumstance, wind, earthquakes, and fire may be happening all around us. Regardless, God will be right there, speaking in His gentle whisper. When the world is screaming, we must listen ever more intently, particularly when our emotions can easily get the best of us.

In your journal, write down any situation in your life that feels like the fire is at your feet or the ground beneath you is shaking. Take a moment to evaluate any emotions that may be causing you to lose perspective. Then spend a few moments in quiet stillness, listening for the gentle whisper of Jesus. Trust that He is speaking comfort and hope to you today.

OUTNUMBERING ANY OPPOSITION

As the final day in court arrives, Tom whispers to Grace, "Do you trust me?"

Puzzled, she answers, "Yes."

Tom adds, "Completely?" Grace gives him a bewildered look. Tom looks to Judge Stennis. "Your Honor, I have one final witness to call—Grace Wesley—and I'd like permission to treat her as a hostile witness."

With Grace now on the stand, Tom begins an all-out assault on her faith. Everyone is completely shocked by his apparent reversal and attack on his own client, but none more than Grace herself. As his words and seeming betrayal now have her in tears, Judge Stennis asks, "Mr. Endler, are you looking to change your client's plea?"

Tom answers, "No, Your Honor. I say she's innocent of all wrongdoing, but I'm asking the jury to find against her anyway. Let's face it—she has the audacity to believe not only that there is a God, but she has a personal relationship with Him. A person like that can't be trusted to serve in a public capacity.

In the name of tolerance and diversity, we need to destroy her, knowing we stomped out the last spark of faith exhibited in the public square. I say we make an example of her and set a new precedent that employment by our government mandates you first must denounce any belief system you have."

Tom continues: "And if someone happens to slip through the cracks and hides their beliefs, we arrest and fine them. And if they don't pay, we seize their property. And if they resist, enforcement is always at the end of a gun."

Stennis brings his gavel down hard and yells, "Mr. Endler! You are out of order and hereby charged with contempt!"

Tom's rant continues, "I accept the charge, since I have nothing but contempt for these proceedings! If we're going to insist that a Christian's right to believe is subordinate to all other rights, then it isn't a right at all. Someone will always be offended. Two thousand years of human history proves that. So I say we get it over with. Cite the law; charge the jury, and send them off for deliberation."

Stennis takes the challenge. "So be it. We will bypass the usual closing arguments, unless Mr. Kane finds the need to further address the jury."

Kane answers, "No, Your Honor. We can ask nothing more."

As the judge dismisses the jury for deliberation, Amy, seated in the gallery for this dramatic conclusion, gets up to leave. A journalist leans in to her and says, "She hasn't got a prayer."

———·———

Tom's risky strategy is to so stack the deck against Grace and her faith, by even her own defense coming against her, that everyone, especially the jury, would see the deep implications this trial might create.

As Christ followers, it does not matter who or how many may come against us. God always trumps anyone, anything, anywhere, any time, in any situation.

> If God is on our side, can anyone be against us? … If God says his chosen ones are acceptable to him, can anyone bring charges against them? Or can anyone condemn them? No indeed! … Can anything separate us from the love of Christ? Can trouble, suffering, and hard times, or hunger and nakedness, or danger and death? (Romans 8:31, 33–35 CEV)

God's Word is quite clear that community among believers is crucial to both our growth and impact. If this were not so, why would we need the church? But there will also be times when even those closest to us will turn their backs on us, and we will have to decide whether we will stand—even alone— just like Grace. As today's passage states so well, even when we feel abandoned by others, we are never alone!

Soak in these truths:

God is for you. God accepts you. God has chosen you. God does not condemn you. God will be certain nothing separates you from Him—now through eternity.

In your journal, write down any lies you may believe that are counter to these statements. Then mark them out and write these truths over them. Why? Because these are true! God says so!

TRUST THROUGH THE TRIAL

Grace sits quietly at home praying, sensing the calm before the storm. Walter is doing what he has done many thousands of times—interceding before the Father for his granddaughter. The phone rings. Walter answers and says, "Okay, I'll let her know." He smiles at Grace and gently speaks, "They've reached a decision." She kisses him on the cheek and heads out the door, and Walter feels a fear he hasn't felt in many years.

Back in the courtroom, Grace makes a point of not making eye contact with Tom. Kane glances over at them with a gloating stare, anticipating yet another win. Judge Stennis asks, "Ladies and gentlemen of the jury, have you reached a decision?"

The jury foreman stands. "We have, Your Honor."

"How do you find?"

Grace takes a breath, realizing her life is about to change forever with a single sentence—either way.

———

As painful and traumatic as this entire situation has been, Grace will never be the same—win or lose. Her faith has deepened and broadened in ways she never thought possible.

No matter the verdict, she will discover Jesus wasn't silent after all; He was hard at work on her behalf and in the lives of all those around this case—Brooke, Walter, Tom, Martin, Amy, Jude, Pastor Dave, and even the Thawleys and Kane. God wasn't distant at all, but right there with Grace through the greatest trial of her life—literally.

> Five times the Jews gave me thirty-nine lashes with a whip. Three times the Romans beat me with a big stick, and once my enemies stoned me. I have been shipwrecked three times, and I even had to spend a night and a day in the sea. During my many travels, I have been in danger from rivers, robbers, my own people, and foreigners. My life has been in danger in cities, in deserts, at sea, and with people who only pretended to be the Lord's followers. I have worked and struggled and spent many sleepless nights. I have gone hungry and thirsty and often had nothing to eat. I have been cold from not having enough clothes to keep me warm. Besides everything else, each day I am burdened down, worrying about all the churches. (2 Corinthians 11:24–28 CEV)

When we're having a bad day or a rough season of living out our faith, this is a great passage to help regain perspective. While we are certainly blessed with so much freedom, our calling and ministry from Christ is exactly the same as Paul's.

Consider Grace's story—a simple, down-to-earth, girl-next-door school teacher who, when her time came, stood up, would not back down, and trusted God through her fear and the scrutiny of even the court system. This is how modern-day Christianity can be lived out. Grace didn't see this coming; she was just being herself. But when the going got tough, she got tougher, relying on the strength of Christ.

We each must be ready. What choice do you believe you will make?

Stepping back or speaking up?

Bowing down or boldly standing?

Running from the flames or walking into the fire?

Today's passage shouldn't create guilt or fear, but encourage and inspire us when our own time is at hand that those who have walked before us have given us amazing examples and blazed a trail of incredible faith.

Take a few minutes to think through Grace's story. Write down your own thoughts about how you might respond to a similar situation. Which parts scare, inspire, or embolden you to stand as she did? Ask the Lord to prepare you, as he did Grace, for whatever comes your way.

SHOW THE WORLD
GOD IS SURELY ALIVE!

Congratulations on completing the forty days of devotionals in this book! All of us involved with this project pray you now have a greater and deeper understanding of what life looks like when you live believing God is surely alive. You can be His living, breathing evidence every day.

We want to encourage you to continue your new habit of spending time with God daily—reading His Word, praying, listening, applying, and growing in your faith. Then take all He gives you and reach your world for Christ. We pray you live out your faith just as Grace Wesley did.

God is inviting you to join Him in His work, so stand strong and show the world He is surely alive in your life!

I pray that from his glorious, unlimited resources he will empower you with inner strength through his Spirit. Then Christ will make his home in your hearts as you trust in him. Your roots will grow down into God's love and keep you strong. And may you have the power to understand, as all God's people should, how wide, how long, how high, and how deep his love is. May you experience the love of Christ, though it is too great to understand fully. Then you will be made complete with all the fullness of life and power that comes from God. Now all glory to God, who is able, through his mighty power at work within us, to accomplish infinitely more than we might ask or think. Glory to him in the church and in Christ Jesus through all generations forever and ever! Amen. (Ephesians 3:16–21 NLT)

ABOUT THE AUTHOR

Robert Noland began his writing career as a songwriter in 1983, penning lyrics for artists such as Glen Campbell, Babbie Mason, Paul Smith, and Gabriel. He then spent the next 10 years as a touring musician and producer. He wrote his first series of Bible studies in 1988 and in 1991 wrote his first Christian devotional book for a para-church ministry.

Noland has since authored over 60 titles spanning across children, youth, and adult audiences. In 1996, he wrote a Christian follow-up booklet entitled *LifeChange*, published by *Student Discipleship Ministries*, which to date has sold over one million copies.

In 2010, he released his first book, *The Knight's Code*, along with *3SG, Men's Small Group Manual* through his own ministry *517 Resources, Inc.* Robert regularly blogs at *theknightscode.com* and speaks at Christian men's events.

Since 2011, he has been a free-lance writer and editor for Christian publishers, ministries, and faith-based organizations. Recent projects where Robert has contributed his writing and editing include:

—*Facts & Trends* magazine (LifeWay 2014-2015)

—*Think, Act, Believe Like Jesus*, Randy Frazee, Zondervan 2014

—*Do You Believe? 40 Day Devotional, (*From the *Pure Flix* film, *Do You Believe?)*, BroadStreet 2015

—*When God Shows Up: 40 Day Devotional* (From the Jon and Andy Erwin film *Woodlawn)*, BroadStreet 2015

—*Living Among Lions,* David & Jason Benham, *W Publishing* 2016

—*How to Live in Fear*, Lance Hahn, *W Publishing* 2016

Regardless of the target audience or mode of delivery via paper or digital, Robert writes what he calls, "practical application of Biblical truth." He lives in Franklin, Tennessee with his wife of 30+ years and has two adult sons.

Visit his web site at robertnoland.com

Notes

Notes

Notes

Notes